El Delirio

The Santa Fe World of Elizabeth White

El Delirio

The Santa Fe World of Elizabeth White

GREGOR STARK *and* E. CATHERINE RAYNE

Edited by Jo Ann Baldinger

School of American Research Press ∞ *Santa Fe* ∞ *New Mexico*

SCHOOL OF AMERICAN RESEARCH PRESS
Post Office Box 2188
Santa Fe, New Mexico 87504-2188

Director of Publications: Joan K. O'Donnell
Editor: Jo Ann Baldinger
Art Director: Deborah Flynn Post
Indexer: Douglas J. Easton
Printer: Thomson Shore, Inc.

Library of Congress Cataloging-in-Publication Data:

Stark, Gregor.
    El Delirio : the Santa Fe world of Elizabeth White / Gregor Stark
and E. Catherine Rayne ; edited by Jo Ann Baldinger. — 1st ed.
        p.   cm.
    Includes bibliographical references and index.
    ISBN 0-933452-52-7 (pbk.)
    1. White, Elizabeth, 1878–1972. 2. Santa Fe (N.M.)—Biography.
3. Women civil rights workers—New Mexico—Santa Fe—Biography.
4. Women art patrons—New Mexico—Santa Fe—Biography. 5. Indians
of North America—Civil rights—New Mexico—Santa Fe—History.
6. Indian art—New Mexico—Santa Fe.   I. Rayne, E. Catherine.
II. Baldinger, Jo Ann.   III. Title.
F804.S253W48   1998
978.9'5605'092—dc21
[B]   98-19878
                                                     CIP

Cover: Elizabeth White with Gelert of Ambleside, ca. 1930.
Photograph by Bachrach. Title page: Elizabeth White dressed as Queen
Nefertiti for a party at El Delirio, ca. 1930.

Printed and bound in the United States of America

Contents

Illustrations

Martha and Elizabeth White on the portal of the original house at 660 Garcia Street, ca. 1925.

Introduction

In the mid-1920s two wealthy New Yorkers, Elizabeth White and her sister Martha Root White, the daughters of writer, newspaperman, and financier Horace White, built a delightfully eclectic estate on what were then the outskirts of Santa Fe, New Mexico. They hired the artist William Penhallow Henderson, one of the originators and shapers of what has become known as Santa Fe style, to design and build their house and lay out the grounds.

The Whites called their new home "El Delirio" (The Madness) in homage to a bar of the same name in Seville, Spain. While sightseeing in Seville's barrio, the sisters repeatedly became lost and kept ending up at that particular bar, from which they were able to make their way back to their hotel. "Whenever we found *El Delirio*," Elizabeth would later explain, "we knew we were home."[1]

El Delirio immediately became a gathering place for Santa Fe's lively community of artists, writers, anthropologists, and archaeologists. Today it is the campus of the School of American Research, a center for advanced scholarship in anthropology and Native American art.

Catherine Rayne with her Afghan hound, Missy, ca. 1955.

On an autumn day in 1993, Catherine Rayne and I made a pilgrimage to El Delirio. As nurse, friend, and companion to Elizabeth White, whom she called "Miss E.," Catherine lived at El Delirio from 1943 until Elizabeth's death in 1972. (Martha had predeceased her sister by some thirty-five years.) We entered the estate from Garcia Street, crossed the parking lot, and passed between the old Martha R. White Memorial Gallery and one of the guest houses. The Gallery—a small, intimately furnished room with a kiva fireplace—was the first house built after the original two-room adobe building on the property was remodeled. In the last year of her life, Elizabeth moved back into the Gallery while the antique furniture in the main house below was being fumigated. After it was done, she didn't want to leave, and it was in the Gallery that she died.

We walked through the small flagstone patio under an enormous catalpa tree, passing an *horno* (beehive oven) near the boiler room and the New York Room on the right. Catherine described the New York Room to me: "The interior was elegant. The crystal chandelier reflected light in the silver lamé of the drapes, bringing to life the rows and rows of books on the walls. Over the fireplace hung a portrait of Elizabeth at three years of age, done by George

The New York Room at El Delirio in the 1960s.

Peter Alexander Healy, painter of royalty. On the opposite wall was a full-length portrait of Martha as Queen Penthesilea, an Amazon queen in Greek mythology."

According to William White Howells, a Harvard University anthropologist and the son of Elizabeth and Martha's younger sister, Abby White Howells,

During and after World War I [Elizabeth and Martha White] bought at least three houses on 55th Street between Park and Lexington, a block east of the house where they were born [in New York City]. Their idea was to prevent the possible building of a new apartment house next to their final residence, number 115. In 1918–19 my family lived in one of these houses, number 127, while the Whites were in France and Belgium.

On their return my father, John Mead Howells, designed the interior of 115. The living room was paneled in wood of a pleasing medium brown, with Spanish style iron grills on the two windows on the street. All the rest was book cases to hold their own and their father's books, except for a fireplace and marble mantle, with Isha's [Elizabeth's] baby portrait above, and a sofa embrasure opposite with Martha's Amazon portrait above.

Elizabeth White with Gelert of Ambleside, one of the first two Irish wolfhounds
purchased for El Delirio's Rathmullan Kennels, ca. 1930.

On finally abandoning New York they kept the house, with their characteristic affectionate generosity, for my own family to live in, from 1934 to 1939 when we moved to Wisconsin, finally selling it just after the war, when the buyer made it over into apartments. The interior of the living room was taken to Santa Fe and put up in a new room in the open space between the two old houses complete with books and portraits. This was not a recreation of the New York Room; it *was* the New York Room, and it was startling, to one who knew it, to step from New Mexico into New York, an extraordinary illusion.[2]

Catherine and I proceeded down the flagstone steps, crossed a graveled terrace—"It was always kept spotless," Catherine remarks. "The gardeners would get down and pick up every last leaf"—and descended to the lower terrace. In front of us stood the main house of the estate, with its distinctive two-storied living room modeled after the adobe church at Laguna Pueblo. To our left was a walled garden with a pineapple-shaped, pink Georgian marble fountain. A huge, graceful cottonwood arched over the patio just beyond.

We entered the house through a long portal, now enclosed by a wall of mullioned windows on the west. During Elizabeth's life, pots of night-blooming cereus filled this passage, and Knut Goxem, the butler, would open the door to the hallway, sniff the air, and announce, "Madam, we will have a blooming tonight." Turning left at the end of the hall, we descended a short winding staircase to the library, now the office of the School of American Research's president.

A bust of Horace White once graced this room, where Elizabeth entertained guests at small dinner parties. The carved door frame has a tropical motif of pineapples and birds, traditional Victorian symbols of hospitality. The floor tiles were copied from the Prado in Madrid. The wood ceiling, carved by William Penhallow Henderson, is painted in earthy red and blue, with floral motifs that match the floor in spirit. In front of a built-in bookshelf there once were lovely filigree grates of wrought iron, which Elizabeth acquired in Seville in 1929. At one end of the room is a *reredos,* an altar screen brought up from Guatemala by archaeologist Sylvanus Morley after an earthquake

Top, the main house at El Delirio in the 1990s, now the Administration Building of the School of American Research; bottom left, a Spanish wrought-iron gate; right, the Guatemalan reredo, *with Gustave Baumann paintings, in the dining room.*

*Catherine's
bedroom in the
main house.*

destroyed the church. "Elizabeth had Gus Baumann [another renowned Santa Fe artist] remove the gruesome crucifixion scene and paint angels with lutes," Catherine said.

Beyond this room we passed through the summer dining room and entered the kitchen, where appliances and sinks stood on opposite sides of the kitchen. One side was the province of Knut Goxem; the other belonged to his sister, Gunhild, the cook at El Delirio.

Returning to the main hall, we stopped at the first room on the left, Miss E.'s bedroom. "I remember seeing her in bed when she was resting, shortly before she died," I said. "Her hair was done nicely, and she was wearing a bed jacket with a mink collar."

"Oh, no," Catherine objected. "Would Queen Victoria have let you into her bedroom? No. And neither would she." But I do remember Elizabeth's bed, which her friend Jack Lambert built from a pair of carved wooden oxen yokes she had picked up in Portugal in 1929. Catherine writes,

> The small bedroom that she inherited after Martha's death was large enough for this bed, over which hung a magnificent Plains Indian shield of that faded red that becomes a soft coral, decorated with blue, white, and black, small beadwork with lovely black and white eagle feathers hanging loosely from the bottom. Beside her bed was a beautiful Cochiti Pueblo drum, which she used as a telephone stand.

A doorway sealed in the back was the base for an Early American extension of ten inches into the room, made into a very useful wardrobe. Two antique chests, one on either side of the lone window, filled one side of the room. The Indian corner fireplace was rarely if ever used, and a large comfortable overstuffed chair was the "settled in" spot that …[one of] the dogs … called his own. Should you decide to sit in it, when the dog arrived, he would surely let you know you should find another seat. If gentle nudges didn't get the word across, the dog would lie facing you with head on folded paws. His eyes would be glued to your face until you very apologetically gave way.

From the bed itself you could see a beautiful early eighteenth-century trastero [cupboard], dating to about 1740. The roseate decorated doors below closed over three very plain drawers. Above, ornate latticed doors protected six drawers, these inlaid with ivory, and beautifully carved. The entrance door and one opening onto the portal were from a collection of doors [William P.] Henderson had found in Central America. The floor was covered with Indian rugs.

This is probably the smallest room in the house, but Elizabeth chose it for her bedroom because it had once been Martha's. The room also contained a little red chair. In her childhood games in New York, back in the 1880s, she used to pretend it was a prairie fire.

Knut's room, next along the hallway, was simply furnished, with one bed, two chests, a rocking chair, and a desk. Beyond it is the room that had been Catherine's, with its elevated floor of wide pine planks, a small kiva fireplace, and a grille with drawers to cover the large steam radiator. Catherine had an old Spanish Colonial bed and a shoe closet, a *nicho* in which she could hang her shoes by the heels. A dressing table, a chaise lounge, a couple of Spanish Colonial chests, and an Oriental rug completed the furnishings in Catherine's day. In the hallway outside the double doors a bougainvillea bloomed under a tinwork skylight.

We retraced our steps back toward the emotional and physical centerpiece of El Delirio: the living room, often called the chapel. It's a spacious room, 25 feet wide and 45 feet long, with ceilings from 16 to 22 feet. Great

Elizabeth in El Delirio's living room, the interior of the "chapel" in the main house.

Indian pots stood on Spanish Colonial trasteros, and a Plains Indian buffalo-hide painting of a buffalo hunt adorned the wall. "Judging from the external aspects," Catherine writes,

> you would say the building was a church, and with good reason. Willie Henderson built it along the lines of the church at Laguna Pueblo. At the far end was a small balcony where an orchestra played for parties and dances. The opposite end of the room was used as a stage for occasional theatrical productions, especially in the early days; in later years the room was in use more often for music.

At Christmas for two or three years the Santa Fe Sinfonietta and Choral Society performed sections of Handel's *Messiah*. More often chamber music was enjoyed, a woodwind quintet, or trios or more of strings. One of the first concerts was Sept. 2, 1953. The program consisted of Sonata No. 6 in G minor by Vivaldi, for oboe, bassoon, and harpsichord, followed by Quintet Opus No. 16 by Beethoven for oboe, clarinet, horn, bassoon, and piano. Elizabeth White was at both the harpsichord and piano. The chamber music happenings went on several years, under the baton of Dr. Hans Lange, until he was no longer able to conduct. These evenings were often followed by a supper party for from 50 to 175 guests. This wonderful room, which provided so much pleasure, was called the chapel.

It also was a living room. At the apse end were at least three islands where groups gathered for conversation, thus robbing it of any barnlike ambiance. The huge Spanish trasteros and two lovely *verguenas*—ornately carved Spanish traveling desks—gave a wonderful Old World atmosphere to the room. The floor was of a cement tile with Oriental rugs here and there. The ceiling was also patterned after a Pueblo church, with aspen latillas in tweed design between the vigas, patterned alternately white, dark blue, and rose red. Two remarkable old tin chandeliers hung from the ceiling with their many bulbs casting interesting shadows. One island near the front door was native furniture made of pine by Willie Henderson, Joe Bakos, and others.

One very interesting French sofa was solely for the Afghans, and the only one on which they were allowed to lie.

Elizabeth White's trust was worth nearly three million dollars when she died. She gave her beloved El Delirio to the School of American Research (SAR), which hosts scholars in anthropology from around the world for week-long advanced seminars and year-long residencies of intensive study and writing, supports work by Indian artists, and publishes books in these fields. SAR built an additional structure for its Indian Arts Research Center to house the Indian Arts Fund collections Elizabeth had worked so diligently to nurture.

Throughout her life, Elizabeth felt great affection for her family: her younger sister Abby, married to architect John Mead Howells; their two children, William White (Bill) Howells and John Noyes Howells; Bill and his wife Muriel's daughter Muriel Gurdon and son William Dean Howells; and John and his wife Kay's daughter, Polly Hayes. Bill Howells visited Elizabeth periodically after Martha's death. Catherine remembers one visit in the summer of

Skywatching on the terraces at El Delirio. From left: Mark Kelly and friend Kitty, Muriel Howells, William White (Bill) Howells, Catherine, and Elizabeth, 1948.

1948: "Bill walked out of his apartment on an upper terrace with his hand extended, pointing to Venus in the midmorning sky. With the help of Dr. Franco Rigola, who was visiting from Italy, he set up a telescope and projected the image onto a movie screen, where it was photographed." (Love of the heavens apparently was a family affair; one of Elizabeth's cousins was married to George Hale, the father of the great Hale telescope at Mt. Palomar in California.)

Elizabeth's grandnephew, William Dean Howells, called Dean, visited El Delirio often with his family in the summers between 1967 and 1972. Dean's wife, Cristina, admired Elizabeth White for the independent, strong, and sensible personality that she was. "She knew what to shrug off. No one else was telling her what was good and what wasn't. But it wasn't that it was good or bad. It was that it was *her* taste."[3]

Catherine Rayne said that, in spite her well-known love of parties, "Miss E. didn't really like to be close to people sometimes. If there was nothing particularly interesting going on in the world, she'd retreat to her reading. She loved her quietude. We'd sit together the whole afternoon in her room, me knitting, she with a book. And maybe a fifteen-minute conversation." Today, that quiet is enjoyed by creative scholars from around the world as they pursue their research and writing projects at the School of American Research.

A view from the roof of the main house, 1928.

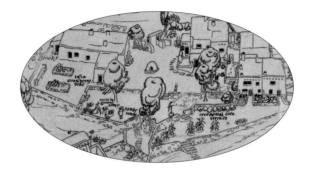

CHAPTER 1

Santa Fe Style

In his charming "Map of El Delirio," Gustave Baumann, one of Santa Fe's best known artists and a good friend of the White sisters, depicted the estate at 660 Garcia Street as it looked in 1927. The main house and walled garden are in the left foreground, the tennis court in the right foreground, and the swimming pool, terraces, gardens, and guest houses at the top of the sloping property, closest to Garcia Street. The "Arroyo de la Tierra Blanca" snakes through the center of the map. Baumann did not confine his drawing to buildings and grounds but also portrayed the kind of life that unfolded at El Delirio by including humorous and intimate details: the tiny figures of archaeologists Vay (Sylvanus) Morley and Joe Spinden excavating "an old pueblo site"; one of the White sisters on the terrace calling Sandy the dog (and being echoed by a parrot on a stand); Sandy himself enthusiastically digging in the prairie dog village; and the mock Mayan pageant held to celebrate the completion of the El Delirio swimming pool, Santa Fe's first. Finally, Baumann enclosed his map within a border reminiscent of a Navajo sandpainting. One begins to see El Delirio as a story told in architectural form whose end, as with the sandpaintings, is a reconnection with first principles.

Gustave Baumann's "Map of El Delirio," 1927.

*Top, the Laguna Pueblo Mission, one of the models for Henderson's design
of El Delirio, ca. 1935; bottom, the newly constructed main house
at El Delirio, 1928.*

El Delirio's walled garden, seen from the dining room, 1928.

The buildings and gardens of El Delirio blend Pueblo Indian, Spanish Colonial, and Moroccan influences and reflect a philosophy in sharp contrast to the individualistic Protestant ethic: the idea of communal living, or the collective housing of extended families and clans. The White sisters' decision to integrate architectural styles on their estate should not be interpreted as a rejection of the Victorian Protestant imagination, however; the mansion they built in Miami, also in the 1920s, was a Georgian masterpiece, far more traditional than El Delirio. But Santa Fe apparently inspired an imaginativeness that broke the Victorian mold. El Delirio evolved as a confluence of Old World royal trappings, Andalusian architecture with heavy Moorish homage, Mesoamerican foundations, Pueblo Indian communality and architectural materials, Spanish Colonial simplicity in furnishings, and New York chic.

In the walled garden adjacent to the main house, a containment pool releases water into a canal, from which it flows into a circular maze and then down a few steps to another pool framed by reeds. The rectangle in the center of the garden is repeated in two progressively larger terraced gardens and then in the outer walk. In design and impact, this space is rooted in Spain rather than England. It eschews the highly trimmed and manicured Victorian style, and its symmetry calls to mind the Alhambra in Granada, one of the finest examples of Moorish architecture. Octavio Paz offers one way of viewing the difference: "It seems to me that North Americans consider the world to be something that can be perfected, and that we [Mexicans] consider it something that can be redeemed."[1] The Pueblo Indians might add that the world is something to be blessed. Of course, the world is all of these things—a fact the White sisters seemed to recognize in their eclectic approach to design.

The local Santa Fe architecture of the early 1900s was typified by the simple, flat-roofed adobe house at 505 Garcia Street, which might be the proto-type for all that El Delirio was built upon. Before the arrival of the White sisters, Garcia Street was a close-to-the-bone community. The original one-and-a-half-room adobe structure on the acre-and-a-half at 660 Garcia was the Whites' first home in Santa Fe. The lifestyle that ultimately evolved at El Delirio combined the simplicity of New Mexican village life with the sophistication of Manhattan, a juxtaposition illustrated by a photo of Elizabeth standing with some of her Irish wolfhounds in downtown Santa Fe. Elizabeth is dressed as if about to set out for a promenade on Fifth Avenue while, behind her, a barefoot boy and his friends look on.

Elizabeth with four of the Rathmullan hounds in downtown Santa Fe, ca. 1930.

The house at 505 Garcia Street, ca. 1928.

A few years before the Whites bought their property, some prominent Santa Fe citizens, concerned that the city's unique character might be lost in the blind rush toward "progress," had begun speaking out about architectural styles. Archaeologist Jesse Nusbaum sketched a history of developments up to that time:

> For nearly two and a half centuries, until about 1850–60, it appears that Santa Fe, like Topsy, just grew naturally. Ditches diverting water from the Rio Santa Fe for the irrigation of tillable fields largely determined the pattern of settlement and road development.
>
> Through all this period of progressive development, a simple regional type of architecture persistently prevailed. The Spanish settlers introduced the adobe brick, and merged certain features of Indian pueblo construction with such traditional forms of their colonial architecture as native materials permitted. Until 1850, at least, Santa Fe appears to have remained completely indifferent to non-regional trends.

After about 1850, a slow insidious trend toward new non-conforming architecture developed. The American military occupation introduced the sawmill and sawed lumber, fired brick, and new forms of roofing that altered appearances. Next, wealthy traders and other residents began to build ornate non-conforming houses like those then in vogue in the East. The advent of the Santa Fe Railroad in the early 1880's ended the excessive cost of importing building materials over the Santa Fe Trail, and soon Santa Fe was indulging in all sorts of building innovations. This foreign architectural trend culminated alarmingly in the first decade of the present century with the introduction and rapid development of varied types of California bungalow in several sections of Santa Fe.[2]

Edgar L. Hewett, first director of both the School of American Research and the Museum of New Mexico, put the debate into a historical and emotional context. In 1917 he gave a talk entitled "Santa Fe in 1926" that framed the discussion over progress versus tradition:

The last decade saw serious changes. It looked at one time as though the old Santa Fe, with its charm of antiquity and perfect adaptation to environment, was destined to give way to something altogether mediocre and in every respect as characterless as the towns of the middle west. But the community became conscious of the loss that was impending ... It is safe to say that the next ten years will tell the story. Whatever the city is to be for all time, as to architectural character, will be determined during this decade.

Hewett went on to describe an aspect of this character, as he saw it, that was the subject of concern:

The two northern streams carried up from Mexico by the priests and colonizers of New Mexico and California in the early 17th and late 18th centuries, respectively, cannot owe their local variations entirely to environment. There is something racial about it. Santa Fe, in its early domestic architecture, was decidedly Moorish. It was Andalusian, with the strong Moorish cast that was imparted to everything in Southern Spain ... The ecclesiastic of Mission

Portal of El Delirio's main house, 1928.

architecture of New Mexico was such a distinct development from the Fran-
ciscan of Mexico as to warrant the permanent name "New Mexico Mission"
in distinction from the arcaded "California Mission."

The world does not afford a finer study in architectural adaptation than
these Missions. First, they display the historic ancestry of the type derived
from Mexico ... Then in a perfectly unstudied way this is merged into the
style of the native Pueblos. The workmen under the direction of the priests
carried out the feeling of their own art with no violence to the foreign style
that was given them. The material was the earth on which they stood and the
forests nearby. Lack of tools except the very crudest, and scarcity of metal prevented finished workmanship. The building is a product of its environments,
raw, crude, virile, imposing its simple strength, and at the same time display-
ing touches of finest aesthetic feeling.[3]

Like Hewett, the Whites saw clearly what was at stake and set about
exerting their influence on the side of creative design, subject to the local style.

They were familiar with the Pueblo, Andalusian, and Mexican architecture that formed the origins of this style, having visited the Indian pueblos of New Mexico and villages in both Spain and Mexico. Elizabeth collected beautiful specimens of furniture and fine antique wrought-iron gates while she was in Spain in 1929. These she integrated into the home along with Southwest Indian crafts, Spanish Colonial furniture, and a rich variety of Southwestern textiles.

At the same time that they were building El Delirio, Elizabeth and Martha bought and remodeled the historic Sena hacienda, a piece of prime real estate one block east of the Santa Fe Plaza. William Penhallow Henderson, whom they had hired to build El Delirio, was in charge of this project as well.

> In its finished form, Sena Plaza comprised 68 rooms and a second floor on the northeast as well as west side of the court. Steel structural members were used in the addition and remodeling, though the appearance of the building belies such technology. Much of the original floor plan was preserved, and with it certain eccentric details. The patio was entirely enclosed, and the portal on East Palace Avenue restored to its Territorial appearance, with closely spaced posts ... One particularly interesting feature of Sena Plaza is the incorporation of round arches in the zaguans [entryways] that provide access to the patio from Palace Avenue and through the north (rear) wing of the building ... Passing through the zaguans, one always is aware of the one form in relation to the other, square within the silhouette of arch or vice versa.[4]

This play of circle and square, which was familiar to the Whites from their travels in North Africa and Spain, also influenced their plans for the land they wished to develop. Garcia Street was a dirt road in the 1920s, with livestock grazing on the hills, and the White sisters fought to keep it that way. The roads around El Delirio were laid out to conform to the contours of the land.

Martha described her vision to Francis C. Wilson, the sisters' Santa Fe lawyer, in a letter dated 1 December 1927:

> With regard to the new tract on the highroad, I have a lovely idea about it and am submitting it to you first before doing anything. Elizabeth likes the idea.

*Clockwise from top left: Entrance to historic Sena Plaza in downtown Santa Fe;
the portal of the original house at 660 Garcia Street, 1920s; herding goats on
Garcia Street in the 1920s.*

It is this. If there is anything horrible it is an "addition" (so-called) laid out like a checker board, which is the only idea that most people have, I suppose to make sewer laying easy. For the sake of sewers they sacrifice every other quality that might make the place attractive. A checker board there on the rising land, as you approach the city, would be horrible and is just what we have been wanting to save the place from. For several years I have had the idea that the way to handle such a thing, at once easy and interesting, would be to take the ground plan of some Spanish city, the layout of which in a general way, conforms with the piece of land, and lay the new streets in that manner, giving them the names of the streets in the original town. This has for several years seemed to me a perfectly delightful thing, always within the possibility of anyone with a piece of open land to develop. Why should we not handle this land in that way, taking advantage of the new museum soon to be erected in one corner, as one focus of interest?

I am sending you under separate cover a guidebook to Spain which has the ground plans of a number of Spanish cities. I had meant to send it to Willie [Henderson], asking him to look at the plans and see what would fit . . . And suggest to us an attractive layout. People of taste, it seems to me, would like this in choosing sites for homes.[5]

The estate itself incorporated many architectural styles in a rich exploration of northern New Mexico's Indian and Hispanic roots. Artist and builder William Penhallow Henderson had a genius for integrating folk design, decoration, and detail into a pleasing whole, respectful of its sources. Through the efforts of Henderson, the architect John Gaw Meem, the White sisters, and many others, a "Santa Fe style" of architecture evolved out of the principle that new housing and commercial property could be built using traditional methods, materials, and designs, and still serve the modern client well.

Much of the careers of Henderson, Meem, and Elizabeth White were dedicated to linking modern Santa Fe with its ancient heritage. All three attempted to give form to their belief that the city could evolve without dissociating from its past. Henderson created integral wholes, whether they were buildings, paintings, or chairs, as models of synthesis. Meem, whose ideas still

*Above, the terraced landscaping at El Delirio,
looking from the roof of the "chapel" to the
original 660 Garcia Street house, 1928;
left, artist and architect William Penhallow
Henderson, ca. 1915.*

dominate the architecture of northern New Mexico, worked to preserve old buildings and bring forth new ones out of that rich, tactile, down-to-earth heritage. Meem designed for the present with a real grasp of how that present would influence the future and an affectionate eye for the simple folk roots of architecture. Elizabeth White gave herself to the world of commerce and institutions that connected past and present, including a viable commercial site (Sena Plaza) that integrated a historical building into downtown Santa Fe business life. Both Meem and White were founding members of the Old Santa Fe Association, an organization dedicated to preserving and maintaining Santa Fe's ancient heritage, and in the 1940s both became members of the city's first formally chartered planning commission.

In 1924 the White sisters formed the De Vargas Development Corporation for the purpose of acquiring and developing land. The legal basis for establishing title to their land was set by the Court of Private Land Grants, established by the US government in 1891 to resolve land title questions resulting from the Treaty of Guadalupe Hidalgo, which ended the Mexican-American War of 1846–48. On the matter of claimants to the land the Whites were to acquire, the court had already decided in favor of the City of Santa Fe. This meant that claims made on this piece of land prior to the Treaty of Guadalupe Hidalgo were not honored.

Letters between the Whites and attorney Frank Wilson describe the process of securing the property from those who had bought it from the City of Santa Fe after the 1891 decision.

Oct. 9, 1924
Dear Miss White:

I have just returned from Albuquerque and desire to advise you that I obtained a quitclaim deed from Judge Hanna covering the tract of land …We can … bring a suit to quiet title on the tract and cause all parties interested to appear and in the final windup obtain title to not less than eighty acres and possibly double that number … [at] approximately seventy dollars an acre …
Yours very truly,
Francis C. Wilson

Martha wrote back regarding two people who had, in good faith, bought tracts to land the Whites now had title to. She brought Wilson's attention to their desire to keep the views as unspoiled as possible:

> How about the bootlegger, K., with the chicken farm? His unsightly mess is right before us always, and we would be interested to know for what we could buy him out. He seems contemplating a windmill, which will make things worse, so the sooner we get a line on him the better.

On 20 November Elizabeth wrote a follow-up letter: "I enclose two checks of $4000 each . . . Will you please buy the K.'s property for us at once. It is a hideous price but we feel that it is MOST important to secure that tract."

In a letter dated 19 January 1926 Wilson informed Elizabeth and Martha of the status of their development:

> The De Vargas Development Company now holds as the owner in fee simple, approximately sixty acres, running along College Street [now the Old Santa Fe Trail], opposite Cuttings, nearly to the top of the hill, but there are a few pieces which we have not yet got in proper shape to claim. The man . . . who owns the K. place, or claims to do so, is difficult to deal with, but I expect to make him a party to the suit in a day or two and think we can bring him to time. I will not pay any exorbitant price for this land, and what we have offered him is twice what it is worth. It is a clear case of hold-up and before I go further with him I am going to see what the result will be of forcing him into court to defend his title . . . I am having Mr. Henderson fence College Street to the extent that we have now obtained a good title, so that there can be no further trespasses upon that much of our land. Do not worry about the K. piece yet, as I think we will be able to make the man see some reason . . . I might state here that the average price per acre of land so far acquired is about $250— which is not at all bad for the average, and I believe that it is worth $500 per acre at this time.
>
> I might state also that there is quite a little boom here in real estate as a result of a number of things which have occurred since you left in the fall.

The Santa Fe Railroad Indian Tours Service is a thing now assured and they have purchased the largest garage here and are now figuring on the purchase of the La Fonda hotel, to be operated by the Fred Harvey System. There is talk—which seems to be quite definite—of some sort of a community center to be created and established here by the Federated Women's Club of Texas on a piece of land lying within the city boundaries on the Tesuque road. Also, yesterday the American Metal Company formally took over the Pecos Mines, and there is to be a very large development as a result of that deal, which will bring to the city of Santa Fe a large increase in new money due to payroll, of the operation, and other expenditures which are likely to be made in this town. In consequence of these things, and other minor matters that are pending, there has been a decided increase in all values. The result of all of this is a great demand for land and houses in this town, unequalled in the 18 years that I have been here.

The White sisters did not always share Wilson's enthusiasm for development in Santa Fe. Regarding the plan of the Federated Women's Club of Texas to bring a chautauqua to the city, Elizabeth wrote to anthropologist Alfred V. Kidder that "Old Santa Fe would vanish before this swarm of locusts."[6]

On 4 April 1926 Martha wrote to Wilson:

Will you, please, arrange to have the dump calling itself a house, on the K. place, razed and carried away . . . If the wood is worth anything as seasoned lumber, all the better. We are inexpressibly relieved that it is settled, and that that region is not going to turn into another shanty town.

The Whites were determined to shepherd a development that would capture the character and flavor of the best of old Santa Fe. Elizabeth kept her eye on general development in Santa Fe and pushed for conservative regulations. In April 1930 Frank Wilson wrote to her, "Last fall the City Council took action restricting all of the end of town down to the Chamisos Arroyo, which is embraced in our tract and the Santa Fe Holding Tract, and excluding business from that section." Just to make sure, the Whites attached covenants to the sale of their property, restricting building style and future conveyances:

> FIRST: That no building…except a private dwelling…be erected…And said dwelling house and necessary outbuildings shall be in the style or form or appearance known as the Old Santa Fe or Pueblo-Spanish style of architecture…no billboards… And no windmill.
>
> SECOND: That no conveyance shall be made or granted of said premises, or any part thereof, to any person or persons of African or Oriental descent.[7]

The second covenant was attached as a matter of course to many of the lands being developed in that part of Santa Fe. In the 1940s Elizabeth White had it removed.

Horace White and Elizabeth White riding in Central Park, ca. 1890.

CHAPTER 2

Formative Years

Elizabeth White was born in 1878 into a world of culture and privilege. She grew up on the posh upper east side of Manhattan, traveled regularly to Europe, and studied the classics at Bryn Mawr College as a member of the class of 1901. But rather than settling into a life of ease, Elizabeth employed her prodigious energy and her other gifts—those of the imagination and the spirit as well as her material wealth—to enrich the lives of the individuals and communities she loved.

The city of Santa Fe, New Mexico, was a particular beneficiary of her generosity. White made her primary home in Santa Fe from 1921 until her death in 1972 and was a community activist long before the term was coined. She loved Santa Fe's land, history, and multicultural heritage, and she worked tirelessly to support and preserve them. She was instrumental in founding the Indian Arts Fund, the Old Santa Fe Association, the Laboratory of Anthropology, the Garcia Street Boys and Girls Club, and the Santa Fe Animal Shelter, all institutions that continue to thrive today.

In the 1920s and 1930s White fought passionately on behalf of the Pueblos and other Native American peoples to resist the official US government policy of forced assimilation. She was an ardent advocate for Native American arts and crafts and the Pueblo Revival architecture that came to be known as Santa Fe style. And she was a devoted friend and gracious hostess who entertained her circle of artists, writers, musicians, anthropologists, and archaeologists at El Delirio.

White was a petite, slender woman whose flexibility and charm, combined with a strong will and a clear sense of values and priorities, made her a force to be reckoned with. "Miss E. was a *real* lady," said her longtime friend, archaeologist Marjorie Lambert. "One of the things I liked best about her was her voice. It was so musical. And when she spoke she had something to say. She wouldn't keep quiet when people were rude at board meetings. I can hear her saying to Mary Wheelwright, 'Now Mary, you *know* that's not true.' Her wisdom, coming out musically . . . She was one of the great women of the Southwest in a very small body. As great as she was tiny."[1]

Some would say that Elizabeth inherited her strength and determination from her father. Horace White was born in New Hampshire in 1834. Four years later his father, also named Horace, moved the family to the Illinois Territory, where he founded the town of Beloit (now Wisconsin). The younger White received a classical education at Beloit College, which his father had helped to establish. In 1853, at the age of nineteen, he became a journalist for the *Chicago Journal*, and two years later began a long career at the *Chicago Tribune*, eventually rising to the position of editor. As a young reporter at the *Tribune*, he met Abraham Lincoln and covered the Lincoln-Douglas debates.

Horace White was proud of his New Hampshire roots and considered himself a true Yankee, shrewd and hardworking; his daughter Elizabeth brought a similar kind of New England vigor to her efforts to help the Southwestern Indians. "They got their iron from their father," said Elizabeth's nephew William White Howells, referring to the three White sisters. Horace White's ferocity was exemplified in an intolerance for the inhumane treatment of animals. In the summer of 1906 he took his daughters to Alaska. On board the steamer from Seattle was a man with a bear that did tricks for money. Infuriated by the spectacle, White bought the bear and donated it to the Chicago Zoo.

White showed considerable skill in pursuing his own economic interests, and as a young journalist he dabbled in investments. His interest in finance dwindled, however, when he became passionately involved in the struggle to abolish slavery. He was acquainted with John Brown, met with him "frequently ... And personally provided him and his sons with Sharps rifles and Navy revolvers."[2]

In 1865 White made a propitious purchase:

On April 14, the eve of an ominous day, John Locke Scripps sold his share of the *Tribune* to Horace White. He made a mistake. The next issue of the *Tribune*, under its reorganized ownership, regretfully found the startling issue which delayed any decline in the paper's circulation. Thousands of people bought copies of the *Tribune* to read the dreadful news of [President Lincoln's] assassination. The huge Hoe press continued to whirl during the next month, as *Tribune* circulation averaged over 45,000 copies. Only the *New York Herald* could claim a wider audience. Buoyed up by this sign of continued prosperity and even more by advertising receipts which topped those of any paper in the West, the *Tribune* owners expanded their eight-column newspaper to ten columns on May 22, 1865, to accommodate the increased advertising. Horace White had made a bargain.[3]

White's prominence in the national scene accelerated after he acquired the *Tribune*. He served in the US War Department under President Ulysses S. Grant and later, in partnership with entrepreneur Henry Villard, invested in the *New York Evening Post* and numerous business ventures, including railroads. He supported the gold standard and wrote in his economics textbook, *Money and Banking*, "It must be borne in mind, however, that all trade is barter, even when the precious metals are employed as intermediaries—the latter being articles of barter also, and possessing the same values as the things for which they are exchanged. *The whole science of money hinges on this fact.*"[4] White believed firmly in the absolute value behind labor and money.

That Elizabeth White inherited her father's sense of absolute value can be seen in the way she began collecting Indian art and crafts in the 1920s.

Although she bargained for the goods she purchased, she did not abuse the relationship between maker and buyer. She knew the objects had an absolute value far higher than what was being offered at the time, and dedicated herself to educating a sophisticated East Coast art market about Indian art so that it might command the prices it deserved.

Left, Elizabeth, ca. 1882; right, Mary Ann Carroll (Nana).

Horace White's first wife, Martha Root Hall, died in 1859 after a brief, childless marriage, and he married Amelia Jane McDougall in 1875. Their first child, Amelia Elizabeth, was born on August 28, 1878. Within a few years two more daughters, Martha Root and Abby McDougall, followed. Elizabeth (as she was always called) was only five years old when her mother died. Horace, who never remarried, was a devoted father. He raised the three girls on what was then the upper east side of Manhattan, on East 55th Street between Madison and Park Avenues. An Irish nanny, Mary Ann Carroll, known as Nana, lived with the family.

The White sisters, ca. 1884: Martha Root White, Amelia Elizabeth White, and Abby McDougall White.

As a girl, Elizabeth was fascinated with the physical world. On a trip to Bermuda when she was thirteen, she wrote to her father,

> I am going to tell you about our visit to the dock yard for I have learned something about machinery ... He showed us a piece of machinery that would cut iron right in two at one end, and at the other end it would punch holes right through solid iron ... We were also taken on board the gunboat "Scorpion" which was made for the confederates the same time that the "Alabama" was made in eighteen sixty-one. But when the English heard what damage the "Alabama" was making they would not let the "Scorpion" go. We went below and a man showed us two great big cannons. There was lot of tremendous shot fastened to the walls, each weighing two hundred and fifty pounds so the man told us.

She went on to describe the range of the guns, the life preservers, and more, in great detail. "I hope I have not tired you with this long letter. But don't you think I have learned something?"[5]

Elizabeth was exposed to the culture of the Old World during her travels in Europe and her studies at Bryn Mawr College. In 1894, at the age of sixteen, she was in Paris, studying French, ancient Egyptian history, geography, and arithmetic. Her sketchbook from that trip includes delicate, detailed drawings of Swiss mountain vistas and folk costumes and two paintings of classic Roman and Greek scenes. At Bryn Mawr she studied English literature, philosophy, biology, psychology, mathematics, Greek sculpture, and languages—Greek, Spanish, French, and German. (Her choices were undoubtedly influenced by her father, who was steeped in classical history and had translated five volumes of Appian's *Roman History*.) She also chaired the De Rebus Club, which invited speakers such as Booker T. Washington to the campus.

Both Elizabeth and Martha were interested in the traditional arts and crafts of their own and other cultures. In college Elizabeth tried her hand at woodcarving; years later, in the 1914–15 edition of *Women's Who's Who in America,* she described herself, among other things, as a woodcarver. Even earlier, it was clear that folk art drew Martha and Elizabeth's attention. In 1893, when Elizabeth was fifteen and Martha thirteen, their father took them to the Columbian Exposition in Chicago. Martha wrote to Nana:

> When we reached the grounds we went first to the Liberal Art building and there we saw an elephant tusk that was all carved with faces and houses and people and flowers, so that there was not a square inch that was not carved, and we saw an elephant's tusk over a yard long. After our lunch, for which we waited over half an hour, we went to a street in Cairo, where we rode on donkeys and had a ride on a camel.[6]

The description conjures the world and values that would predominate in Martha's and Elizabeth's activities throughout their lives. The image of a carved ivory tusk presages descriptions in their later writings of classical Greek pottery, fine folk furniture from Spain, Portugal, and Central America, American Indian pottery and jewelry, and East Indian, Middle Eastern, and Egyptian musical instruments. Elizabeth collected in each of these areas.

A story about a mouse that Elizabeth wrote while she was at Bryn Mawr reveals a characteristic sensibility, a subtle feeling for the little things in life.

> There is what is called "a blower" shutting my [fireplace] grate, and behind this screen the mouse lives an eccentric life. I have seen him only once (thank heaven!), but I have heard him so often that I feel acquainted, in a distant way, as one feels acquainted with Lohengrin or President McKinley. On the occasion of our meeting he was much the less embarrassed, but as I was studying Empedocles, and he was playing a game, he had the advantage.
>
> Have you ever seen a small boy going along the street and tracing the irregularities of the house fronts? He runs up a few doorsteps and down into area-ways and dins with a stick along iron railings. That is what the Mouse was doing. He outlined the bookcase and then the breadbox. Next he turned the corner by the door and, hastening around the worktable, disappeared into the fireplace. His manner was not in the least furtive, and though he must have seen that I had discovered him (for, truth to tell, I instinctively drew my feet into the chair), his poise did not forsake him; in fact, he seemed to take particular pains not to cut any corners.

A letter from Elizabeth that appeared in the Bryn Mawr journal was signed "A.E.W.—All Elegant Whims." Her attentiveness to the small details of life, which would later find meaning in the world of Indian art and craft, was combined with a dramatic sensibility and a fiery political will.

Elizabeth's passion for folk art was but part of her decision to move the center of her world from New York to Santa Fe in the 1920s. Whether or not she felt the same discontent with the East as did others of the time, she left New York to find a place that would engage her whole imagination.

At the start of the twentieth century, American enterprise was rapidly creating new wealth and new standards of success. Definitions of worth and value, whose reference points had long been located in European traditions, were being turned on their heads. Elizabeth White had been brought up with old ideas of cultural achievement, yet she was in close contact with the new wealth and values of industrial America. When she came to focus on Indian and Spanish arts and crafts, she recognized the intrinsic value that arose from the cultures themselves and not necessarily from the brilliance of an individual artist.

The White sisters had grown up just around the corner from Tiffany's, a monument in the world of "taste." Henry James wrote of Tiffany's:

> [It] presents itself to the friendly sky with a great nobleness of white marble. One is so thankful to it, I recognize, for not having twenty-five stories, which it might easily have had, I suppose, in the wantonness of wealth or of greed, that one gives it a double greeting, rejoicing to excess perhaps at its merely remaining, with the three fine arched and columned stages above its high basement, within the conditions of sociable symmetry.[8]

Only three hundred years earlier, the land on which Tiffany's stood had belonged to another people. Within that span of time there developed, in what came to be New York City, a society far removed from one in which sociable symmetry expressed itself naturally.

*From left, William Dean Howells, William White Howells,
Abby White Howells, and Horace White, ca. 1908.*

James asked the question, To what do objects of good taste refer? He answered that good taste was "present, for reference and comparison, in a hundred embodied and consecrated forms" in Europe.[9] Elizabeth White discovered another source in the Southwest. From her childhood home so close to Tiffany's, arbiter of high-culture American taste, she would journey to New Mexico and encounter cultures whose "taste," if that word can be applied, was so embedded in a religious vision of life and world that the objects it produced revealed something of the human origins of sociability, delight, and usefulness in made objects.

William Dean Howells, a friend of Henry James—and Abby White's future father-in-law—examined the troubling aspects of American business morality in such novels as *A Modern Instance* and *The Rise of Silas Lapham*. One of his characters expressed an increasingly popular attitude toward nature:

> I never saw anything so very sacred about a big rock, along a river or in a pasture, that it wouldn't do to put mineral paint on it in three colours. I wish some of the people that talk about the landscape, and write about it, had to bust one of them rocks out of the landscape ... I say the landscape was made for man, and not man for the landscape.[10]

Howells struggled with his unease about the egotism of American business culture. "For fifty years …[Howells] had been optimistically content with 'civilization' and its ability to come out all right in the end …'Yet,' he wrote, 'I now abhor it, feeling it is coming out all wrong in the end unless it bases itself anew on a real equality.'"[11] Howells concluded that a moral commitment to community saves humankind from destruction. This was a view shared by Elizabeth and Martha White, who eventually would come to live in a community of rich historic and contemporary resources and commit themselves to preserving and developing those resources.

Between 1901, when Elizabeth White graduated from Bryn Mawr, and 1921, when she and Martha decided to settle in New Mexico, industrialization and urbanization were rapidly transforming the face of the United States. For a time it looked as if the old order, though threatened, would somehow carry on as before. All that changed with the First World War, but in 1900 there was still enormous optimism.

For Elizabeth, the first two decades of the new century included travel to Europe, Guatemala, and New Mexico; an unhappy stint as an unpaid essay reader at Bryn Mawr; graduate work in Anglo-Saxon and sixteenth-century literature; a volunteer job at a Manhattan trade school; and service as a nurse in Belgium during the Great War. The three White sisters were actively involved in the women's suffrage movement, participating in marches and demonstrations and socializing with suffragist leaders.[12] Jane Addams, founder of Chicago's Hull House, visited Bryn Mawr in 1912, when Elizabeth worked there as a reader, to lecture on the right to vote. Her essay, "The Modern City and the Municipal Franchise for Women," held that without the full participation of women the modern world would lose whatever social genius of the past had brought it forth, and so lose the ability to revitalize and care for its own. "[Woman] would bear her share of civic responsibility," Addams wrote, "not because she clamors for her rights, but because she is essential to the normal development of the city of the future."[13] Elizabeth and Martha's move west brought them to a region whose recent pioneer history had created a more egalitarian relationship between women and men. In this setting, the

White sisters were able to see broad possibilities for their engagement in society, gain new insights into themselves, and find ways to express that understanding.

Elizabeth's diary for the years 1911 to 1915, a book with space for only five lines per day, provides a glimpse of her life before the move to New Mexico. In the spring of 1912 she participated in a suffrage parade and sorted papers at her office at Bryn Mawr. In the evenings she read Trollope and Chesterton. During that summer she knitted, swam, typed letters for her father, kept an eye on the progress of Woodrow Wilson's campaign, attended a reception hosted by her father's golf partner, Andrew Carnegie, and followed the exciting World Series of 1912, when the Boston Red Sox beat the New York Giants, 4 to 3.

Elizabeth first traveled to New Mexico in August 1913 to visit her former Bryn Mawr classmate Alice Day Jackson and her husband, Percy, at their ranch near Wagon Mound, a tiny, dusty town in the state's northeastern plains. The Jacksons introduced Elizabeth both to the Southwest and to many of the individuals, including the eminent archaeologist Frederick W. Hodge, who would later become her associates. Her New Mexico diary entries read:

8/13—Started for New Mexico at 10 pm. Shall do some more mechanical drawings when I get back.

8/15—Reached Wagon Mound at 11:55. Percy's ranch quite perfect.

8/16—Learning to ride—no rattlesnakes. Cattleman's name for cows = "she-stuff."

8/17—Mr. Hodge has written. His plan involves four days on the train— General horror!!!

8/18—No ride. Everyone overhauling tents and packing. PERHAPS I can get a hat in Santa Fe.

8/19—Took No. 1 for Santa Fe. Met by deputation of archaeologists—Mr. Hodge seems the nicest.

8/20—Very full day. Went to the Museum—thousands of archaeologists. Met the wonderful Mr. Nusbaum.

8/21—Had to arrive at Grants at 3:30 am. Spent the night in a freight car. All baggage gone on. Must stay till tomorrow. Took a walk with Percy

*Top, the Hodge survey party near Grants, New Mexico, 1913. From left:
Sylvanus Morley, Alice Jackson, Elizabeth White, F.W. Hodge, Mary Bulkley,
and Percy Jackson. Bottom, a page from Elizabeth's 1911–15 journal.*

and had a pencil game party—before supper. All 3 archaeologists are double stars. F. W. Hodge, Sylvanus G. Morley, Jesse Nusbaum. We were too sleepy to go to the [dance] hall.

8/22—Got up at 5:15. Started with two wagons. Two horses and prairie schooner at 8:30. Crossed the lava flow after passing San Rafael. Lunched in a little grove and met a cloud burst—in the middle of the road. The country gets more beautiful the farther you go. Camped at the end of Canon Cebollita about 6:00.

8/23—Got up at 5:00 and moved camp back to the golden cliffs. The arches. Stayed to examine the ruins and did not find the lunch we left. Very mad but soon appeased with food. Climbed the mesa for the sunset. Found an aquarium in the rocks full of pollywogs, etc.

8/24—Late breakfast 6:30.

8/28—Very early start got us back to Grants in time to dress (!) and catch the train. Heavenly country. Dined at Albuquerque and got back to Santa Fe about 1:00 am. Nicest birthday in ten years.[14]

In February of 1914 Elizabeth traveled to Guatemala as the guest of the Mayanist Joseph Spinden. Throughout this period, her interest in archaeology and collecting was growing.

Martha's diary for those years contained fuller descriptive passages and offers insight into the way culture, art and craft, and sensory richness resonated with her personality. Her account of a 1911 family trip to North Africa and Europe began with their arrival in Algiers:

June 13—Arrived Algiers around 12:00 . . . Lovely government park—palms and cacti. Rubber trees etc. . . . houses built of [stone] or brick and plastered with mud which dries out white. Whole town white and clean. No smoke. Arabs very handsome. Wear their rags in great dignity. Saw many veiled women. Drove to native quarters and walked through streets 5–8 feet wide. Beautiful doorways with ornamental frescoes of roses etc. worked in the dried mud.

While in Italy the family attended the Siena Palio and watched the various guilds bring their horses into the cathedral to be blessed before a race. Martha described the procession:

June 30—Perfect uproar rising from the streets all the time—bells ringing, donkeys braying, voices. July 2—Finally we wandered up to the Plaza in front of the Cathedral and waited for something to happen. A little boy wandered up with post cards and said they were to bless them (the horses) right away. So we hurried down to the Church. The pages in dark red costumes—sort of Henry VIII hats were already there. A very handsome horse brought in— scared to death. Very pretty little horse, winced when struck by Holy Water . . . Rushed—had tea . . . Then scampered to the Campo and saw the thousands pouring in . . . Most orderly crowd. No elbowing.

At six the mounted gendarmes cleared the track. The procession started. The Contrada we had seen, preceded by a brass band, a horseman with the city colors—Black and White—at end were a double row of children with laurel wreaths—Horses had other bridles on. (In procession they had ostrich feathers on their heads.)

The Quail [guild] won by about three lengths . . . I went right down to the Contrada of the Quail to see what was happening. Painted torches were being put out on the houses and lit. The entrance to the Church was decorated with little paper flags and a huge crowd surging in and out to see the banner they had won in there. A procession of men and boys formed when the Palio was brought

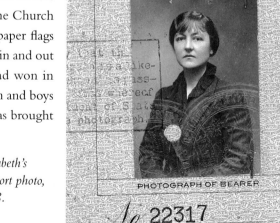

Elizabeth's passport photo, 1918.

out with other banners which they twirled. Later a brass band joined them playing The Animal Fair. They marched through the quarter running down the hills. Later on the girls of the district joined in three or four abreast surging—all very jolly.[15]

This spectacle of collective social life at its most celebratory and expressive was one of many that captured Martha's imagination. In Ireland, in 1914, she wrote that their host told them "amazing tales of Hunt Balls" and "regaled us with marvelous stories of wraiths, faeries, witch doctors, banshees, etc."

There are numerous links between the White sisters' experiences in Europe and the life they would begin to create for themselves ten years later at El Delirio. Martha's diaries demonstrate her appreciation for the sensory qualities of nature, art, and archaeology and for the spirit of rural folk culture and its connections to a living past. She was fascinated with ancient and traditional social celebrations that were preserved before her eyes and loved their more genteel manifestations such as fancy balls and parties. She reveled in the joy of sport and loved dogs and horses.

After Elizabeth's trip to New Mexico in 1913, only two things inspired emotion in her diary entries. One was her growing interest in archaeology; the other was the Great War. In an article entitled "The Queen's Hospital, The Ambulance de L'Ocean of La Panne, Belgium," Elizabeth later described meeting Madame Marie Depage, the wife of Dr. Antoine Depage, who had opened a state-of-the-art hospital at La Panne in collaboration with the Queen of Belgium:

[Mme. Depage] came to America to ask for funds to promote the work . . . As all the world knows, Madame Depage paid for her devotion with her life, being one of the victims of the Lusitania. She was last seen helping other women to adjust their life-preservers. Then she sprang into the sea. But like John Brown, "her soul goes marching on," for her name has ever since been a force in America with which to coin money for the needs of the Belgian wounded.

Having thus known and worked for the interests of La Panne from its beginning, I felt I had but one desire, on coming to France in the spring of 1917, and that was to visit it and see it for myself.[16]

Elizabeth went overseas as a Red Cross volunteer in St. Valery, France, in June 1916. Her father wrote to her that same month, "My dear and precious daughter, Thank-you ever so much for your [letter and] ... post card showing the place where you live. I keep the latter on my writing table so that every time when I look up my eye tells me that you are working to relieve human suffering in a distant land." Exactly three months later, on September 16, 1916, Horace White died. Elizabeth went home for the funeral but returned to St. Valery in April 1917, accompanied this time by Martha. Elizabeth served as a volunteer at La Panne between 1917 and 1918, was decorated for her service by the Queen of Belgium, and continued to volunteer in a Paris hospital through the end of 1918. She wrote Abby about the journey to the coastal town of La Panne:

After we passed Clermont we began to see the refugees. I have never seen anything so tragic. The whole countryside fleeing for the second time. I don't know which is sadder, the old, old people or the children dragging

Elizabeth (left) as a Red Cross volunteer in Belgium, 1917 or 1918.

along on their poor tired legs. They were taking everything they could with them, their carts, their horses, their cattle, flocks of sheep. A real exodus. After we passed Auxerre they flooded into the train. There were 15 in my compartment at one time not counting a little old dog (eleven years old his mistress said) who had lost his teeth and a huge cat in a basket curled up and sleeping like a true philosopher. A lot of these creatures were fleeing for the second time. I can't describe the effect it makes on one to see such a procession moving along the roads. It is simply heart rending. They don't hurry. They just move along with resignation and constantly the soldiers were helping carry the babies or push the baby carriages . . . I could not help crying.[17]

In their letters to Abby, who was managing their financial affairs, both Elizabeth and Martha combined news of their daily routine with advice about the White estate. Martha wrote,

As regards your keeping the accounts do as seems to you best of course, but be sure you are not giving yourself too much to do. It is exacting work, as they have to balance the books to a penny all the time. When the estate is settled I suppose the books will be open to inspection if requested by the courts. Mr. K could tell you about this. I know you can keep accounts like a good one. But it takes a long time to chase a missing 10 cents and it is entirely for you to say whether you want to burden yourself, with your other responsibility, or insist on a complete monthly statement from Mr. K. He would of course give it.[28]

Behind all this discussion of finances was the inheritance the three had received from Horace White's estate, probably amounting to a yearly sum of about $55,000 each (financial records are unavailable for verification). It was this income that would allow Elizabeth and Martha to set up an independent and original lifestyle in Santa Fe.

San Ildefonso Pueblo in the 1920s.

CHAPTER 3

Indian Lands and Indian Health

Even before Elizabeth and Martha White arrived in Santa Fe, they had became involved in a furious battle being waged in Congress over Pueblo Indian land rights. In 1921 New Mexico Senator Holm Bursum had introduced legislation, known as the Bursum Bill, that would make it easy for non-Indian settlers to obtain Indian lands. In opposition, the White sisters and their colleagues in the Eastern and New Mexico Associations on Indian Affairs (EAIA and NMAIA) proposed a more moderate solution, one that would protect Indian lands and at the same time recognize the complexities of Spanish grants, Mexican grants, US territorial rule, and conflicting Supreme Court rulings. This compromise would be called the Lenroot Bill.

The White sisters approached the Pueblo land problem with the same fervor they had used to raise funds for the hospital in La Panne during World War I. Martha took over New York's Metropolitan Opera House for a performance of *Othello* to benefit the EAIA. Elizabeth corresponded regularly with the EAIA and NMAIA lawyers involved in the fight to protect Pueblo lands.

"Harvesting Wheat," linoleum block print by Tesuque Pueblo artist Juan Pino, ca. 1925–30.

The EAIA, which Elizabeth helped form in 1922, worked to protect the Indians from the unbridled exploitation of business interests and from a policy determined to bring the Indian into white society. But it fought equally to protect individual tribal members from abuses at the hands of tribal authorities. In one case, a public health nurse took a stand against a Pueblo governor on behalf of a woman who had been beaten by her husband. In another case, members of the Indian rights organization examined a woman whose chest had been scarred by the lieutenant governor of the pueblo she had married into. He had allegedly rubbed her chest on the lock of a door for "telling tribal secrets."[1]

It is important to understand how moderate Elizabeth White's approach was in the context of the times. She did not agree with the federal government's goal of total assimilation of Indians but, like her EAIA colleagues, recognized a moral responsibility on the part of non-Indian citizens of the US toward the Indians. Convinced that "the United States government collectively represents higher practical ideals towards the Indians than do the states in severalty,"[2] the EAIA fought several congressional bills that would have turned over responsibility for Indian welfare to the states.

Between 1887, when the Dawes Severalty Act made it possible to allot Indian lands to individual tribal members, and 1933, when John Collier became the US Commissioner of Indian Affairs and terminated that act, American Indians lost more than 87 million acres of land.[3] In New Mexico, the lands question was complicated by the history of Spanish and Mexican land grants and by the status of Pueblo lands during the period when New Mexico was a US territory (1848–1912).

The Bursum Bill of 1921 granted title to non-Indian settlers who had claims on Indian land if they could show continuous possession of that land for ten years, with no compensation for the Indians. Bursum pushed the bill through the Senate on a voice vote, reporting falsely that the lawyers for the bill had been selected with Indian approval.[4] He had the support of Secretary of the Interior Albert B. Fall, who later resigned during the Teapot Dome scandal. Fall heated up the political climate in support of a rash solution by threatening to evict the three thousand non-Indian settlers on Indian lands.

Word that Pueblo lands were threatened spread across the Southwest. Santa Fe artists and writers, among others, raised a storm of protest unlike any the Indian Bureau had ever seen. Such famous local personages as F. G. Applegate, Mary Austin, Jozef Bakos, Gustave Baumann, William P. Henderson, Will Shuster, and Carlos Vierra joined nationally known figures including D. H. Lawrence, Carl Sandburg, Maxfield Parrish, and Edgar Lee Masters in the protest.

The Bursum Bill failed in the House of Representatives after a last-minute appeal. It was at this point that Elizabeth White became involved. While the NMAIA was being organized, she enlisted the help of several influential anthropologists and others on the East Coast and formed the EAIA to fight the Bursum Bill and pursue broad Indian welfare activities.

Two camps would emerge on the side of the Pueblo Indians: the moderate EAIA and NMAIA, and the visionary John Collier and his American

Indian Commissioner John Collier at the Tohono O'odham Reservation, Arizona, 1940.

Indian Defense Association (AIDA). The former, believing that congressional hostility toward Indian welfare made it judicious to proceed carefully and slowly, supported a plan to reconcile Indian claims with the purchases and acquisitions of Pueblo lands by non-Indians that had been made in good faith at a time when US laws allowed the Pueblos to sell their lands. In contrast, Collier's plan essentially held Indian claims as inviolate and would compensate those good-faith purchases by non-Indians with payments from the US Treasury. Collier managed to alienate almost everyone who did not whole-heartedly share his views, and Congress was no exception. Charles H. Burke, who served as Commissioner of Indian Affairs in the 1920s, tried to please both sides and ended up pleasing neither. Collier attacked his policies openly.

The NMAIA's annual report for 1921–22 provides a sense of what the Bursum Bill was about:

> Last April the San Ildefonso Indians asked us to look into the water situation. After going over the ground we reported to the Agent, and possibly due to our activities the Agent and Government Farmer notified the settlers on the Pojoaque Creek that the Pueblo was to have the water for two days every week. In August we made another investigation. We went with the San Ildefonso Indians to the head of the Pojoaque Creek and saw them close all head gates as arranged by the Agent. By three or four o'clock in the morning the water should have reached San Ildefonso. But the next morning we found that of the thirty head-gates closed the previous afternoon, only two had remained closed.

Other NMAIA activities in 1921–22 included contributing winter rations to San Ildefonso and Tesuque Pueblos, which had suffered from the summer's drought, providing counsel to the "Chief" of Acoma on the land issue, advising Jemez Pueblo on railroad rights-of-way and Santo Domingo Pueblo on highway rights-of-way, protesting federal policy that interfered with Pueblo religious life, and other matters of general Indian welfare and policy. "One interesting experience," the 1921–22 annual report mentioned, "was that of having the Northern Pueblos call a council at Mrs. McComb's house.

We were not notified beforehand and the twenty-odd delegates arrived quite unexpectedly. They brought a complaint of stock trespasses. We drafted a letter to the Agent and the Indians were authorized to collect rent from the owners of the stock."[5]

The organization also provided assistance to individuals:

Thomas [Vigil] was an artist at Tesuque, but in the fall of 1922 he contracted trachoma and almost lost his sight. Thanks to Mrs. Warren, the Government trachoma specialist has been in this district nearly all summer, and Tom's eyes are almost well. But last year Tom's income was reduced to zero. When Miss White of the Eastern Association was here she agreed to buy all the pottery Tom's wife would make. In a small way we tried to do what the Museum has done at San Ildefonso in raising the standard of the pottery makers. Each week this girl's pottery is improving, so that now the family has a nice little income.

Inez Tafoya is entirely blind in one eye and was nearly so in the other. For several years he had been receiving rations from the Government from a fund known as that for blind and indigent Indians. This fund was suddenly done away with, and Inez and his sister who was also nearly blind, were suddenly left without anything. Inez could not get work, he had no land, his father had sold it. We secured rations for him, we told the trachoma specialist about him, the Council at Nambe said as soon as he could see he should have a piece of land. Then we heard that every time the oculist went to Nambe, Inez went to the hills. So we went to see Inez. After lengthy argument, supported by the Governor, Inez agreed to come in with us and his eye was operated on. The oculist says the sight in that one eye will improve steadily.[6]

The crux of the disagreement between Collier's forces and the EAIA over the Bursum Bill concerned the statute of limitations. If non-Indian settlers had purchased or otherwise acquired Pueblo land while New Mexico was a US territory, federal law upheld their title to that land. This was based on the idea that "the real owner cannot sit by forever and neglect to assert his claim.

He is supposed within the limitation period to throw off the squatter; or to bring suit against him; or to make his title good in some way."[7]

Collier's forces contended that it was not fair to hold that "the Indian has lost title to his lands because he did not forcibly throw the settler out or bring a law suit—when he did not know the English language, was baffled by the complex procedure of the Courts," and was poorly represented, misrepresented, or not represented at all. "To hold that Indian inaction in such case had lost him his land would be a ghastly travesty of justice."[8] On the other side, the EAIA believed that, like it or not, those laws had applied since the signing of the Treaty of Guadalupe Hidalgo in 1848, that most of the settlers who had acquired title to disputed lands had done so in good faith, and that the US government had a moral responsibility in such cases to compensate the Pueblo Indians for lost lands.

In 1923 John Collier organized an All-Pueblo Council to discuss the Bursum Bill—possibly the first all-inclusive organization since the Pueblo villages united to eject the Spanish in 1680. The next year he held another meeting at which he cast the EAIA as foes of the Indians and his organization as the only trustworthy one. The EAIA members were furious, and not a little hurt. Collier's divisiveness here was in part a response to the earlier EAIA compromise with Congress, when, without consulting Collier, the group's attorneys Francis Wilson and Roberts Walker had negotiated with Congress on the Bursum Bill in a closed-door session, attempting to cut their losses. The Lenroot Bill was the result.

Collier's profound historical vision and Wilson's and Walker's political savvy ended up completely polarized. An exchange of letters captures the mean spirit of the conflict. On 17 April 1923 Wilson wrote to Collier:

> As evidence against you, your letters referred to cannot be improved upon, and so far as I am concerned they will pass as proof out of your own mouth of your undisciplined and unprincipled mind and temperament.
>
> Underlying your whole attitude concerning the Lenroot substitute and myself there is one phase which has at last become apparent to me. Instinctively and apparently fundamentally, you are opposed to any orderly process

of law and those who are called upon to enact laws and to administer them. You resent bitterly any effort on the part of those whose minds have been trained in the school of constitutional government and the proper administration and interpretation of law to impose any restraint along those lines upon your views ... A person constituted as you are with the vicious and destructive limitations imposed upon your mind by a prepossession in opposition to law and forms of law, is impossible, and a danger and a detriment to any cause which must be worked out pursuant to the constitution and laws of the United States. You are yourself, therefore, the embodiment of as dangerous a feature in the fight for the Indians as the foes with whom we have been and are now fighting. Any association with you must in the long run be discreditable to the Indians and to their cause and to the people, who without a full realization of your actual frame of mind, embark with you upon such a fight.[9]

Collier wrote back on 22 April:

My Dear Mr. Wilson:

Your letter of the 17th did not reach me till yesterday. I find it distinctly interesting, though I must first point out that it is irrelevant to the subject we have been corresponding about. Your contention is that you are a man who believes in the orderly processes of law and I am one natively hostile to law-and-order, constituted authority, etc.—an anarchist or bolshevist by temper if not by profession.

The Pueblo situation would seem to indicate that you have the thing all mixed up—that I am a law-and-order person and you are what you call me. For I am pointing out that the Pueblos have legal title to property; that the Lenroot Bill proposes to take this property away from them ... I am pointing out that the government has a continuing responsibility toward these Indians, and am insisting that a Government undertaking has the same force of binding moral honor that an individual's undertakings have, whereas the Lenroot Bill violates such a Government undertaking and guarantee without even so much as a "Beg your pardon" to the victims.[10]

Collier was sensitive to the deeper issues in the matter, including the fact of inequality in power, but was unable to grasp the need to work, negotiate, listen, persuade, and build coalitions based on mutual respect. Elizabeth White said of him, "I do not know him personally but from what I hear it may be difficult to get him to act tactfully."[11] She had encountered Collier secondhand for the most part, although both were members of the Committee of One Hundred appointed by Interior Secretary Hubert Work to consult and advise on Indian policy. Maria Chabot, a key organizer of the Santa Fe Indian Market in 1927, worked for both the EAIA and John Collier and said, "He made people mad. He was an artist turned politician. It inhibited his art and didn't do much for his politics."[12]

White might have understood what Collier was striving for ultimately, for she herself wrote, "The spirit of the bill is that due process of law is not enough for the Indians. They must have something higher, and more generous than due process of law."[13] What she could not abide was Collier's unruly challenge to authority, an authority she herself wished to reform. That authority was colonial and was summed up in a simple definition in the final Bursum Bill, which created the Pueblo Lands Board. The bill said, "[I]n the sense in which used in this Act the word 'purchase' shall be taken to mean the acquisition of community lands by the Indians other than by grant or donation from a sovereign."[14] In other words, unless Indians had been given the land or had purchased it from a colonial authority, it was not theirs.

The controversy over the Bursum Bill affected the long-standing friendship of Elizabeth White and Elizabeth (Elsie) Shepley Sergeant, a journalist and a member of AIDA, whom White had known at Bryn Mawr. On 14 August 1923, at the time Collier was organizing an All-Pueblo Council to discuss the Bursum Bill, White wrote Sergeant in some distress about Collier's methods:

> As far as we can find out, [the AIDA lawyer] and Collier are going to present a bill for the Pueblo's endorsement on Aug. 25 and Roberts Walker [the EAIA Eastern lawyer] arrives on Aug. 27. I have written him begging him not to get the Indians pledged to some bill that we may not be able to agree on after all. It is not like him to behave that way and I can't understand it.

After the major combined effort against Bursum, White wrote to Sergeant indicating that she felt things were well in hand and that the government officials with whom they were dealing, although possibly incompetent, were no contest for them.

Commissioner Burke had been alarmed by Interior Secretary Fall's attempt to heat up the controversy by threatening to evict all non-Indian settlers. Burke was afraid the settlers and Indians would take up arms. Elizabeth White and her friends, who were closer to the scene and knew the spirit of negotiation to be alive, viewed Burke's dramatics as scare tactics. Elizabeth was sure everything would turn out well and wrote Sergeant to that effect in November.

Between that letter and the next, the compromise Lenroot Bill was drafted by EAIA lawyers who believed that the climate in Congress was far too hostile to get everything they wanted. Collier was kept out of the negotiations. Sergeant wrote an article on the Bursum Bill for *New Republic* magazine in which she described the EAIA as standing "first upon the claims of white settlers."[15] Shocked and angry, White write to Sergeant, "If anything we have done seems to justify your writing as you did I wish you would let me know."[16] Sergeant responded:

> I think I am the person to be shocked and grieved by your letter. How can you say or think that I have misrepresented your motives? I did not touch on the question of motive in my *New Republic* letter, indeed deliberately excluded from the argument all personal relations or equations …What I tried [was to] clarify in objective terms the fundamental divergence of the two groups or societies on the LEGAL aspects of the question …
>
> The legal question, naturally, cannot be resolved by you or me. Either the Indians have title, or they have not, to these lands. Both petitions are arguable and are argued by men of high integrity. If our societies have not the wisdom to effect a compromise beforehand, which will be acceptable to all—I think as I have always that it was and is possible—then the courts will have to decide the question, and it is likely to be decided extremely; and either extreme solution, for the Indians, or for the settlers, is likely to work injustice to one side.

I believe that if the courts establish or if your bill through its Commission establishes the settlers' titles to the lands in dispute, as based on statutes of limitation, these same settlers will get everything they want, over the hands of such devoted people as you, who will be powerless, in that instance, to achieve the practical justice for the Indians that you desire.

White replied, "It is indeed quite useless to write, therefore, I will not comment on the inaccuracies in your last letter. This is merely to state that I have received yours, 'and contents noted,' as we say in business."

By this time Collier had backed off from a sweeping solution and agreed to the compromise bill, which would grant non-Indian settlers title with twenty years' continuous possession and proof of title, or thirty years' continuous possession without proof of title. His lawyers insisted on adding a provision that tax records should be used as evidence of possession—a stipulation that would be largely ignored by the Pueblo Lands Board that decided these questions.

It was Collier and not Elsie Sergeant, however, who was the main target of Elizabeth's ire. In a response to Sergeant's *New Republic* article, Elizabeth wrote opposing Collier's plan to develop a commission which would confer "with the Pueblos for voluntary surrender of such Indian's claims as are not necessary for the communal integrity … Only extreme ignorance of the ways of unscrupulous white men in Indian territories would provide such a broad and easy road for 'the white steam roller.' "[17]

Meanwhile the Indians attempted to communicate their viewpoint, which took into consideration the other's point of view as a legitimate part of the story. Sotero Ortiz spoke to the question at the All-Pueblo Council in January 1924:

When a man comes to buy a piece of land and has extra land the Indian sells the piece of land that is under cultivation only and the one who buys makes a document extending into all that land that is vacant and that is not legal … I am still young, I myself know of some of the sales that have been made in the Pueblo of San Juan under those terms … There was a man who sold about

3/4 of an acre and now the man who is on that land is claiming from the road that goes from San Juan to Alcalde. From that road to the east end of the grant. The land that is above the acequia is still community property, there is not one person alone who has the right to sell that land. Only the governor with the approval of his assistants, the principals, would have the right to sell that land and he has not sold it. Our friends who are living within the grant are feeling a little bit angry with us. They claim what they think is theirs and of course they have a perfect right to defend what they think is theirs. If they are claiming something which is just we will secure that but until now we are claiming something which is sacred. We are not doing any harm to any single person and our wishes are not to do an injury to anyone else.[18]

Attorney Roberts Walker viewed the matter in a strict legal framework. In response to an AIDA brief, he wrote that he did not support paying the Indians for settled lands:

As taxpayers, we violently object to paying compensation for a razed, incorporated town, for expensively improved ranches, for church property or for railroads. But says the "brief," we shall not disturb these holdings, if only the Indians are compensated for the "farming value of these sites." ... Once more, as taxpayers, we object a) to paying for anything a second time and b) to paying today's prices for something obtained over 25 or 35 years ago.[19]

In what might be read as a plea to get back to basics, Pablo Johnson of Laguna Pueblo wrote to Elizabeth White on 9 April 1924:

The Council also expresses its deep gratitude to you and the Eastern Association for the help you have given us. We appreciate more than we can say all that you have done for us. It makes us feel safe to know that we have such good friends back east and the Great Spirit will bless you for helping us poor helpless Indians. All that we Indians ask for is justice and a square deal and we hope that you will stand by us until the whole Pueblo Indian question is settled and we Indians get a square deal.[20]

Just a few days earlier, on 3 April 1924, Elizabeth had written to Frank Wilson, "I don't much like Bursum's latest version of our bill but if you lawyers think it best to shove it through I will be guided by you."[21]

In the end, Roberts Walker, one of the main architects of the Pueblo Lands Act, revealed both his sincerity and good will, and his ultimate inability to imagine a settlement that understood the Pueblo position. He wrote to the editor of the *Forum* on 19 February 1924:

> Conceding, for the nonce, that the Indian Bureau has been misdirected and unintelligent; that our past treatment of Indians has been a crime; that our present treatment is, worse than a crime, a blunder; and, for their civilization, folk-lore, art, song and dance, no less than for our mishandling of their lives, that we owe them a huge debt; conceding all this and more, one question impends: "In what coin should we pay that debt?"
>
> And I answer: In little village or community schools, not vast boarding-schools where several tribes are huddled and drilled. In tools, supplies, and industrial advice always within reach, but never forced upon them. In sympathetic tolerance toward their dress, dances, tribal routine and ceremonies. In a clear code of offenses, published to all Indians (vice the present method, where the superintendent largely makes up his laws as he goes along). In ampler and abler medical advice, with trained nurses and the best of supplies at call everywhere.
>
> In short, without proselytizing or openly "Americanizing" them, by making our own civilization and beliefs so real and so inviting that they will in time—no hurry—gladly come over to us.
>
> With consciously setting out to turn them into dull citizens—dull, because driven and disillusioned—I have no patience whatever. But they will hold fast to that which is good in our civilization and, eventually, come unreservedly into it. Poor splendid anxious peoples! They must finally join us for we cannot join them.[22]

This letter provides a fair picture of the best humanitarian intentions linked, unhappily for the Indians, with a belief in the manifest destiny of white

American civilization. Given the history of active hostility to Indian rights, the Pueblo Lands Act could have been worse. John Collier backed off for the time being. Elizabeth White, who did not share Roberts Walker's sense that wholesale acculturation was necessarily the final goal for Indians, turned her attention to arts and crafts, an avenue affording entry into the mainstream economic system by means of an occupation consistent with traditional Indian practices and values. The arts became a way for many to adapt and still relate creatively to their cultural heritage.

Indian health care in the 1920s and early 1930s was generally of poor quality. Some government doctors worked on the reservations because they had lost their credentials due to drunkenness, sex offenses, or other problems. Hazel Fredrickson, who studied the Indian Health Service in 1929, took a couple of young Indian women along as interpreters at various reservations. "These women were honest," Fredrickson recalled. "And they were afraid. They were afraid of the doctors *and* the Indian superintendents. When I went to interview one or the other, they were afraid of being left alone in the doctor's offices."[23]

In this climate, Elizabeth White became an advocate for Indian health care. She was no stranger to nursing, and in 1924 she undertook a study of trachoma on the Navajo Reservation. A major cause of blindness in warm parts of the world, trachoma is a highly contagious disease spread by flies. In a handwritten note dated 20 February 1925, Elizabeth told Francis I. Proctor that she had "spent the entire summer making investigation at [my] own expense . . . for 35,000 Navajos, one in four infected. Recommend a lab in Albuquerque for study of trachoma."[24] Proctor, a Santa Fe resident, headed a study on trachoma for the Indian Health Service under Commissioner Burke. Elizabeth pushed him continually to exert his influence on the government to become more active in combating the disease. In October 1925 Burke ordered all BIA boarding schools to keep records of students who had trachoma.

The EAIA and its affiliates decided the health problems of the Southwestern Indians were far too serious to wait for the Washington bureaucracy to move. In 1924, EAIA reported, 72 percent of the children at Santa Clara

Pueblo were affected with trachoma. The organization began funding public health nurses, working with the "consent and approval of the government."[25] In 1924 EAIA funded a nurse at Española to work with the northern pueblos; the next year they funded a nurse at Zuni Pueblo, west of Albuquerque. In 1927 nurse Molly Reebel was sent to work at Jemez Pueblo; a couple of years later the governor expelled her for siding with a woman who suffered physically in a marital dispute. By 1931 Reebel had moved to Nava (now Newcomb, New Mexico), and nurse Elizabeth Forster was stationed at Red Rocks, farther north, on the New Mexico–Arizona border.

During the Depression years the EAIA, and to a large extent Elizabeth White herself, were responsible for funding these positions at $200 per month plus expenses. The EAIA had to discontinue the position at Red Rocks in 1933, and the Indian Service took over the position at Nava. In 1934 John Collier, by then Commissioner of Indian Affairs, asked Molly Reebel to work

at a government station at Navajo Mountain, a remote site about ninety miles from the nearest hospital. This position too was funded by an "anonymous donor"—Elizabeth White.

During the years they worked on the Navajo Reservation, Reebel and Forster reported some remarkable experiences. They treated trachoma and tuberculosis, assisted in childbirth, and dealt with medical emergencies such as trauma and injury associated with rural life. Their reports give a picture of the reservation just before and during the first part of the New Deal that was lively, humorous, tragic, and personal. At this time, medicine was changing dramatically for the Navajos. Sandra Schackel wrote:

Tact, patience, and persuasion were necessary to convince Indians that Anglo medicine could provide a safe alternative to traditional health practices. Reshaping attitudes was a delicate process at best, one in which many dominant Anglo attitudes and values were gradually superimposed over Indian customs.[26]

In one of her first reports to the EAIA, Molly Reebel described some of the difficulties she encountered:

You may have an urgent request to go at once and see someone anywhere from one to ten or twelve miles distant, who is very ill and who wants to go to the hospital. You rush frantically to get there over the world's worst roads perhaps to find that while the messenger has been coming for you, some other member of the family has sent for a Medicine Man and organized a sing and by the time you arrive the patient is all decorated with feathers, ashes and paint, and about to begin, and will not be ready to go to the hospital for four days, at which time you are wanted to return and take the patient to the hospital; and you return home, vowing that you will answer no more long distance calls.

However, the very next call you may find someone sadly in need of hospital care—who is more than willing to be taken in, which makes up for the former useless trip.[27]

The nurses' living conditions were spartan. Margaret McKittrick, a principal field worker for the EAIA, wrote to Elizabeth White about a winter visit to Forster when the temperature dipped to 18 degrees below zero. "In spite of the handicap of no dispensary, and terribly cramped living quarters, she was carrying on, and attending to a number of patients. We had a very merry supper, and slept in sleeping bags with our feet practically in the oven."[28]

Forster wrote, as did Reebel, of a growing respect between nurses and Navajo medicine men. In a letter to McKittrick she recalled:

When I came here a year ago I soon realized that the Navajos hereabouts expected to find me antagonistic to their religious customs and were slow to consult me about illness until the medicine man had failed to help, but gradually they are showing more confidence in my good will and often notify me that they are having a sing and invite me to attend. Sometimes I am invited to practice medicine with the medicine man, sometimes am asked to await the conclusion of the sing so as to be on hand to take the patient to the hospital. I am surprised and gratified to find my medicine men friendly and often cooperative. One of them tells me with a serious twinkle that he is glad to have me attend his sings and see good medicine practiced.[29]

Indian Bureau policy changed rapidly under the direction of John Collier. The EAIA and NMAIA were involved in useful transitional projects aimed at alleviating suffering and providing adequate services. One of the more significant efforts of this time, in terms of results, was the training of Indian nurse's aides. Nurse Reebel was asked to participate in one such training. Her description of the class members' health brings home the conditions existing at the time: "During the first week of the Institute, I spent three days getting family history from each girl for the physical record. Our finds were not particularly happy as out of our group of 95, we found 26 active trachomas; five positive T.B.'s, and two suspicious cases; two heart cases; and ten arrested T.B.'s."[30]

Students were taught about baby care—"give baby proper food, be sure that it has two bowel movements each day and plenty of fresh air and sunshine daily." They were also taught how to make furniture out of old boxes and cups and candlesticks out of tin cans, how to make an iceless ice box, and how to mend broken screen doors and windows.

Many Indian nurses and nurse's aides seemed to be able to conjoin this new knowledge with a profound respect for life. Catherine Rayne, who worked alongside many Indian women during this period and later, recalled, "Indian nurses were very caring. They didn't just barge in and 'do a treatment' but told the patient about what they were doing and explained it to them."

Elizabeth White at the 1929 International Exposition, Seville.

CHAPTER 4

Indian Art

Elizabeth White believed that Indian art had a vitality not found in European art. Her friend, the anthropologist and Mayanist Herbert Joseph Spinden, captured its spirit in this story:

> I once inquired of a woman of Nambé how she would begin making an embroidered mantle. "First of all," she said, "I would feed cornmeal of all colors to the butterflies, because they know how to make themselves beautiful."[1]

White, and others like her, recognized that objects produced in an aesthetic tradition of reverence toward life become more than objects, for they are imbued with spirit. Much of what passed for art in America, these individuals felt, had lost the spirit of art. In this belief they were influenced by the Arts and Crafts movement fathered in the second half of the nineteenth century by the English craftsman and philosopher William Morris, who held that industrial design and industrial production take the soul out of an individual's relation to material. As Morris's contemporary, William Crane, put it, "The very producer,

"Two Snake Dancers," watercolor by San Ildefonso Pueblo painter Oqwa Pi, ca. 1925–30.

67

the designer, the craftsman, too, has been lost sight of, and his personality submerged in that of a business firm, so that we have reached the *reductio ad absurdum* of an impersonal artist or craftsman trying to produce things of beauty for an impersonal and unknown public—a purely conjectural matter from first to last."[2]

Elizabeth and Martha White knew the value of art from their education, their travels, and their collections. Having grown up in the international marketplace of New York City, they also knew something about marketing art. In the early twentieth century, Indian arts and crafts were generally regarded as specimens of cultural life, ethnographic curiosities for scientific examination. Elizabeth's purpose in opening a shop for Indian arts and crafts in New York City in 1922 and organizing the 1931 Exposition of Indian Tribal Arts, also in New York, was to present this work as art, not ethnography, and to create a mass audience for it.

Elizabeth was particularly instrumental in developing a market for Indian paintings. She befriended a few Indian painters in the early 1920s, notably San Ildefonso painter Abel Sanchez, whose Indian name was Oqwa Pi. Like most Pueblo painters of the time, he worked with watercolors. These works became a major focus of Elizabeth's collecting and the subject of several shows. Non-Indian artists and writers like John Sloan and Oliver LaFarge saw this kind of art as truly American and felt it connected them to a natural, native psyche. In contrast to European art, which had taken many directions, Indian art stayed close to nature and the central experiences of humankind. Dorothy Dunn, one of the first art teachers at the Santa Fe Indian School in the 1930s, encouraged her students to look to their traditions, such as ceremonial dances, for inspiration, for the aboriginal cultures of the Southwest continued to live in accord with their ancient traditions well into the twentieth century.[3]

Elizabeth and Martha White believed firmly in fine workmanship and artistic integrity. They deplored the pressures on Indian artists to make cheap products in response to demand from an indiscriminate audience, and they recognized the value system that gave birth to Indian arts and crafts. In *The Spirit of Folk Art*, folklorist Henry Glassie spoke of the threat to artistry that a mercantile culture presented:

Collecting is one of the means people use to confront and overcome a world lacking in direct, intimate connections. When ... design separates from making, when artists separate from users and users separate from artists, when things threaten to fall apart, what lies in peril is not folk art but art itself. Industrial artifacts become at best pictures of art, and workers become tools. Fine artists create mere fashion. Folk artists create anemic souvenirs. The result is not popular art. It is not art.[4]

In 1922 Elizabeth opened an Indian arts and crafts shop called Ishauu in New York. (Though it sounds "Indian," the name was derived from the nickname she acquired from her young nephew, Bill Howells, who called her Isha instead of Elizabeth.) Located on Madison Avenue, the shop carried treasures of Indian art and craftsmanship that Elizabeth had collected since her 1914 trip to Guatemala. She articulated both her intent and her standards in a letter to a Wisconsin social worker who wanted to help Indians by brokering their beadwork. Elizabeth, who owned some fine pieces of Plains beadwork, evidently felt that the samples she had received were not up to par: "I am sorry that the things you sent on to my shop were not in the class of material that is sold here. Have you anything of their own traditional design and workmanship? ... I am very much interested in what you are doing as it seems to me the real way to help the economic difficulties of the Indians."[5]

Ishauu, which changed its name to the Gallery of American Indian Art in 1931, never made a profit.[6] Though there were some informed buyers, many shoppers were looking for mere curios, such as the individual who wrote requesting "some interesting black pottery jars from San Ildefonso" to use in making a lamp.

An Ishauu employee sent Elizabeth the following report on customers:

One Afternoon (To the tune of "Barging into Ishauu's")

One large pleasant man, whiskered and wearing rubbers. "A friend of General Custer's Cousin." Knew the Wooly West in the old days, but would not teach in the "Guv'ment schools" because there was too much political machinery. Looked around—"thank you for letting me look."

Three large women—all nice—two with bustles or their equivalent. Looked at bracelets. Will come back. One is regular patron.

One woman, very pleasant, though looked like boiled owl. Wanted present for 1-yr.-old baby. I suggested Katchina doll, (for decoration). She said would suck off paint. I said could keep where could not suck. Did not want. I suggested bright red rug for nursery—could keep when grew up—babies like red. Yes, maybe. Rug might do, but was not sure. How about hand-hammered spoon? Maybe. Would come back soon—wanted something unusual.

Two fat men, wreathed in smiles, and oozing good nature. "I have 20 minutes in which to buy a bracelet." Mrs. Cross wangled him in her efficient and angelic manner. He bought one.[7]

"Isn't it cute—for a present, I mean?" Cartoon from the New York World, 1929.

In 1928 Elizabeth began to plan an exhibition of Indian arts to be held in Paris. She wrote to several friends, all of them influential anthropologists, including Alfred Tozzer at the Peabody Museum at Harvard, Frederick W. Hodge at the Heye Museum of the American Indian in New York, and Alfred V. Kidder at the Carnegie Foundation, asking them to support the Paris exhibition. Its purpose, she explained, would be twofold: to encourage European interest in Indian art and, through this interest, to stimulate American appreciation. Ultimately the Paris exhibition did not materialize, but Elizabeth's efforts led to a subsequent Paris show—the International Colonial and Overseas Exposition—for which she donated many items.

Elizabeth showed her private collection of Indian art at the 1929 International Exposition at Seville, Spain, hosted by the American Consulate. The exhibition was held in a single room, approximately 600 feet square, in which Native American art and artifacts from the Southwest, the Northwest, and the Plains were displayed. Paintings, ceremonial objects, clothing, and other materials hung on the walls. The floors were covered with rugs, and a miniature tipi was exhibited in a fireplace. The items included a case of jewelry, twenty-two paintings, four pottery bowls, two terra cotta bowls, and two cases of ceremonial and everyday items such as a bone drill, headdresses, blankets, rugs, pipes, toys, bows, spears, a knife, and a drum. Elizabeth insured the whole for $5,000. A young woman from the gypsy barrio of Seville served as a tour guide, attired in traditional Navajo dress. At least 3,000 people a week came to view the exposition, which remained open for more than a year.

At such exhibits, it was the custom of the Spanish king and queen to select one object apiece for themselves. "They chose two of my best pieces," Elizabeth later told Catherine. "He took a beautiful Plains Indian war bonnet, and she took a large squash blossom necklace." Elizabeth asked for a photograph of the king, Alfonso XIII, wearing the war bonnet, but her request was never fulfilled. "Evidently he has been so busy in governmental affairs that he has not had the time or inclination to go through this operation," Thomas E. Campbell, US Commissioner for the Seville exposition, wrote to Elizabeth.[8]

Elizabeth donated the exhibit to the US Bureau of Indian Affairs. Shortly thereafter, BIA Commissioner Charles J. Rhoads, a personal friend of hers, received a request to take the materials to the International Colonial and Overseas Exposition in Paris. Elizabeth concurred, but asked to save a few pieces for the International Antiques Exposition and the Exposition of Indian Tribal Arts, both of which opened in New York in 1931.

For the International Antiques Exposition, Elizabeth ordered numerous new objects from traders and included items from her existing collection to fill out the show. "I have taken a space on the second floor at the Grand Central Palace," she wrote to Rhoads. "It is ten by twenty feet and I shall arrange it as an early American room using Indian rugs, pottery, beadwork, baskets, etc. as Indian decorations. I think we shall start a new fashion yet." According to a press release,

> This exhibit was arranged for the Bureau of Indian Affairs by Miss Amelia Elizabeth White, at the request of the Commissioner of Indian Affairs, Charles J. Rhoads. The booth, which was designed by John Mead Howells, the New York architect [and Elizabeth's brother-in-law], will represent an early American colonial room with antique American Indian textiles, pottery, baskets, etc., used as decorative material. The plan is to show how Indian art objects may be used as interior decoration.
>
> The finest pieces in this collection, Miss White stated, will be a part of the larger Exposition of Indian Tribal Arts, which will open in the Grand Central Art Gallery in the fall. The Exposition will include, however, not only fine examples of antiques, but also the work of modern Indian artists and craftsmen, from thirty tribes now living in the United States.[9]

The "early American room" Elizabeth designed, with its beautiful pottery in antique cabinets and its colorful Navajo rugs and wall hangings, was an attempt to bring the pleasure of things made with feeling and spirit into the home.

The Exposition of Indian Tribal Arts opened in December 1931 at Grand Central Galleries in New York and incorporated F. W. Hodge's suggestion that Indians should be invited to demonstrate their culture and craft. Ten Pueblos

Top, the "early American room" at the International Antiques Exposition, New York, 1931; bottom, clipping from the New York Sun, *6 March 1931.*

and two Navajos made the trip to New York, where they danced, demonstrated crafts, spoke to the public, and saw the sights. Elizabeth White was the motivating force behind the exposition. The timing was terrible—the public would not attend such an exhibition in large numbers until 1940—and suggests the extent to which White and her colleagues in New Mexico were insulated from the worst effects of the Great Depression. Nevertheless the exposition was a concentration of energy and scholarship in Indian arts and crafts on a scale that had never been seen before.

In their introduction to the book produced by the exposition, John Sloan and Oliver LaFarge wrote:

> Do not blame the Navajos, or any other Indians, for letting themselves be debauched into curio-makers. They are very poor, they have to make sales. If a barbarian market insists on gewgaws and "quaint souvenirs," they have to make them. If we will provide a demand for good things, the supply will appear immediately. It is to help create just such intelligent demand that this exposition is organized.[10]

Elizabeth devoted herself to this end, carefully choosing and arranging the objects to be displayed. In June 1931 she traveled to the Mescalero Apache, Zuni, and Navajo reservations to acquire art and artifacts for the show. She had a particular design and feel in mind that were guided by her own sense of taste. Hers was not the impersonal motive of the market, but a personal vision of arts and crafts.

The exhibition, which included both prehistoric and postcontact objects, was heavily weighted toward Southwestern, Alaskan, and California Indians, with a few items from Plains tribes and prehistoric Midwestern mounds. Other North American Indian tribes were not well represented, perhaps because since European contact their culture and art had been uprooted to a much greater degree than had occurred in the Spanish Southwest.[11]

The Exposition was not informed by a critique of colonialism as found in contemporary art. Its non-Indian organizers were looking as best they could at original source material that was related to traditional life and values. What was said about this work played an important part in educating the art-buying public and promoting the status of Indian art. "The Indian artist deserves to be classed as a Modernist," Sloan and LaFarge wrote, "...but his modernism is an expression of a continuing vigour seeking new outlets and not, like ours, a search for release from exhaustion." They continued,

From the pottery one sees the trail leading directly to the modern Pueblo painters. In pictures and in pottery, one is faced by the problem of symbolism, how much is meant to be interpreted, how much pure esthetic design. The answer probably is that it's all one. Potter and artist draw their spiritual sustenance from their tribal life, and that life is all a design, a dance and a ceremonial, from birth to death, and through all the ramifications of daily life; it is a whole, individuals are part of a pattern. The deer and the rain design and the unit derived from a butterfly, are used on jars and pictures, they are set deep in the life of the artists, they appear in other forms, still patterned and controlled, in the dances. Of course they are conscious of their symbols, but their whole life is charged with symbols, from them, inevitably they draw their aesthetic patterns; the significance is quite different from what it would be for us, or for Navajos, who use true symbols only with specific interest.[12]

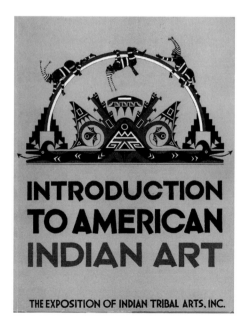

In her contribution on Indian poetry, Mary Austin said:

[The Indian] thinks of poetry as evoking [the spirit power of natural things] and the making of a poem or the making of any beautiful thing as an act of spiritual communion with the Powers, by whatever name he calls them. So there is a song when the newborn child is held up to the light, a song for the corn planting and one to bring the deer down from the mountain; a song for the building of the house, for the cure of the sick, for the making of the bow, for the soul in departing. Friends of the Indian are often accused of "poetizing" the Indian. But the truth is that this is what he has done for himself, done it so completely that our failure to follow him on to the poetic level at which his important processes take place is the chief reason for our failure to understand him.[13]

As the exposition opening neared, plans were made to send dancers and artists from San Ildefonso Pueblo, including potters Julian and Maria Martinez and painters Oqwa Pi, Awa Tsireh, and Tonita Roybal, and Elizabeth commissioned Oqwa Pi to make a tri-panel mural for the show.

When Oqwa Pi arrived in New York, he spoke over WOR radio:

I am so glad to stand here before this Broadcasting Station. I do not really understand how it is done, that the sound goes over my country of New Mexico and we Indians do not know it. It is really fun for us Indians to be here in New York City, place where the rest of my brothers had not seen, to see this tall houses like [cliff houses] of New Mexico along the Rio Grande where my ancestors had lived. I and the rest of my people are here in New York City to present ourselves, so that people will know who we are and what we are here for. Also how we make our living. Our principal works are farming and painting pictures and making pottery.

The exhibition in the Central Art Galleries of this city was formed by our white friends and the Eastern Association of Indian Affairs in order to get the people of our country to understand that there was art in the American Indian. Little of it was done in the past years. Finally our friends got more interest in our works and they also want you people interested in our

*Top, Oqwa Pi in Thunder costume, Santa Fe, 1919; bottom, mural panel
(painting on canvas) by Oqwa Pi, 1931.*

arts and crafts, that is our real American art, that we have here in our own United States for this is what we may call genuine American art. I am also glad to tell you that we are accompanied by Maria Martinez our Southwest potter maker and Tonita Roybal. These two Lady are known to be the far best along this kind of work. We will bring a song to you. Goodby my white friends. Oqwa Pi.[14]

Moris Burge, a fieldworker for the NMAIA, accompanied the two Navajo guests, Nez Bitsidee and Ushkay Begay, to New York. Many years later he talked about this "extraordinary experience":

The Navajos spoke no English. I spoke only a little Navajo ... It was a super deluxe trip. We had a private car on the Santa Fe Chief, arranged by Miss White. We stayed at, I think it was Grand Central Hotel, where we had most of a floor and a private dining room ... They put us on the top floor. We had thought the Indians would want to be on the ground floor but it didn't bother them at all ... I went with them to the Empire State Building. We were on the top balcony ... The two Navajos were in one corner laughing their heads off. They were pointing to the Chrysler Building, laughing. All the rooftops were flat except the Chrysler. One of them said, "Look, it's a Navajo hogan."[15]

In a letter to Oliver LaFarge, Burge described how New York had impressed the Navajo visitors:

I have just returned from a trip to the Navajo Reservation with Margaret [McKittrick Burge]. We visited Nez Bitsidee at Sa-Nos-Tee, and learned ... the details of his triumphant return from New York. He and Ushkay Begay arrived at the Trading Post on Christmas Day, while a Christmas feed, attended by some three hundred Navajos, was in progress. Bitsidee was prevailed upon to describe to the assembled his adventures in New York, and I doubt if he needed much persuading. According to the best traditions of Hyde Park he mounted a box outside the store, and addressed the crowd. Mr. Foutz conservatively estimated that he talked for three hours, describing all that he had done since leaving the reservation, and answering innumerable questions ... "The Navajos," Bitsidee explained, "might believe the reservation to be large, but compared to the rest of the world it is no larger than a dot." To emphasize this he made a small circle with his thumb and forefinger. Everything he saw was beyond his expectations. He was especially impressed by the battleship and, of course, the ocean. "The buildings were taller than the highest pine on the mountains. So many were the people in the streets that it was impossible to tell whether you were coming or going."

He was very favorably impressed with the white women ... [and] apparently astounded to find that they all smoked, but believes they have just as much right as men. One of the Indians asked if he had learned to dance in white man's style. He replied that he wasn't sure, but when his feet had become sore he managed to keep them out of the lady's way.

The sea water has made Bitsidee famous for miles around. When we took the bottles from under the seat in the Pullman, the sand which had been put in the bottom of the gallon jugs was disturbed, and four tiny white sea creatures appeared. This caused tremendous excitement at the time, and Foutz told me that one of the fishes had survived. Bitsidee first showed the precious water to a chosen few, allowing his wife to take some. She washed her hands in it, threw it on her face and hair. This was just as the two Navajos had done at the sea. The medicine men were also permitted to perform a similar rite. The shells were shown, but apparently none was given away. One old medicine man asked Bitsidee how long it would take him to go to the sea in a wagon to get four barrels of water and a load of shells. He was told three years, and decided not to undertake the journey.

A six-day sing with sand paintings was given for the water, for which I understand both Bitsidee and Ushkay Begay had to pay twelve dollars, or half of their earnings in New York. Some of the water was given to the singers. It will be used for rain making ceremonies during the summer.

Apparently the bringing of the water to the reservation has caused considerable consternation among the river Indians, who profess a belief that their section of the reservation was once under the sea. They fear that because this water was brought back the sea will return. When young Foutz told me of this, I thought it was probably the talk of a few of the Shiprock Indians. A few days later, however, I was talking with Sam Drolet at Bernard's Trading Post. Two Navajos who were sitting in the office, when they learned that I had been to New York, told Drolet the same story. The floods which will inevitably occur this spring will probably be due to the imprudence of Bitsidee.[16]

A Navajo Phase III–IV "chief" blanket, ca. 1890–1900, collected by Elizabeth White and donated to the IAF in 1927.

Convinced that the tourist trade was degrading the quality of Indian work, Elizabeth White and her colleagues sought to educate the buying public, expose more people to Indian art, and control the direction it took. They collected and preserved older specimens, supported individual artists by commissioning and buying work and providing technical assistance, and educated the artists and the marketers closest to them. They also attempted to get the government to institutionalize all these forms of support through an Indian Arts and Crafts Board.

A 1935 NAIA bulletin on contemporary Southwestern Indian arts and crafts described how the group viewed its efforts:

When the Eastern Association on Indian Affairs first undertook a definite campaign for the improvement and encouragement of the art of the southwest Indians, there was no other systematized or organized effort being directed to this end . . . [The EAIA] set itself the task of reviving certain of the

Indian arts which had so deteriorated that the modern productions bore little relation, outside of the remnants of technique, to the beautiful old specimens to be found in museums.

However, in this work, as in all its work, the Eastern Association on Indian Affairs insisted in retaining first of all an eminently practical point-of-view . . . [T]hey felt that no matter what the aesthetic value of a given craft, it would be a waste of time and effort to encourage the large majority of Indians to produce solely for aesthetic ends, and from the point-of-view of the Indians it would result in an effort which would bring only discouragement. So in approaching any given problem in the campaign to revive a craft it has been a policy first to inquire into its economic value to the tribe concerned, into sources of raw materials, and into possible markets. Then to ascertain what defects in workmanship or material might prevent a ready sale of any given ware with the purpose of eliminating them if possible.

While insisting on the practical approach, the Eastern Association on Indian Affairs, and more lately the National Association on Indian Affairs, has also given full consideration to the effect of its work in the arts and crafts field on the morale of Indian life. They realized consistently that this stimulus to Indian culture could have important results in maintaining tribal self-respect and raising it to a higher level, that it could increase tribal coherence, and engender in craftsmen a pride in the past achievement of their people, arousing a desire to carry on the finest traditions in technique and design.

Keeping these ends in view, the National Association on Indian Affairs, cooperating with the Arts and Crafts Committee of the New Mexico Association on Indian Affairs, has for the past two years with varying success, carried on arts and crafts projects on the following reservations: Navajo Reservation, Jicarilla Apache Reservation, Mescalero Apache Reservation, San Carlos Reservation, Picuris Pueblo. They have been active, but less intensively so in many other of the Rio Grande Pueblos.[17]

One major effort in the arena of direct education was the design project of the NMAIA Arts and Crafts Committee, funded by Elizabeth and Martha White. The project's fieldworkers, Moris Burge and Margaret McKittrick Burge, brought photos and drawings of older designs in jewelry, textiles, and pottery to artists, Indian traders, and Indian schools in an effort to revitalize the great traditions that seemed threatened by tourist demand for cheap souvenirs. In addition, through the auspices of the EAIA and NMAIA, Mary Cabot Wheelwright and her niece, Lucy Cabot, worked with the Du Pont Company on the East Coast to develop a set of aniline dyes that would match the colors of native vegetable dyes and educated the traders about their use.

Margaret McKittrick and Elizabeth White saw their task as that of educating the traders, who acted as ultimate arbiters for what constituted a good piece within their own locale. Earlier, in a letter to trader Joseph Schmedding of Keams Canyon, Arizona, Elizabeth had written, "I am sorry you have no Navajo silver at present. I am not at all interested in the tourist grade of silver. I only sell what the Navajo makes for himself or for other Indians. Anything of that nature, rings, earrings, bracelets, necklaces, buttons, buckles—that is the sort of silver I have for sale. I will be greatly obliged if you will keep my needs in mind."[18]

Their efforts bore some fruit. A few traders responded heartily to the ideas and carried them on into the next decades. Others also responded with favor, as in this letter to Margaret McKittrick Burge from E. B. Dale, superintendent of the Charles H. Burke School in Fort Wingate, New Mexico:

> First, allow me to express my appreciation for the use of the silver work which we have used in our silversmith shop and now have copies of various pieces.
>
> We have greatly enlarged our weaving department and have a large number of girls now at work almost entirely on antique or old type weaving: however, they are now able to produce larger pieces and practically all rugs being made are of the 3 x 5 size. Our girls work out their designs using your photographs as examples and are doing this work in water color and crayon before attempting to weave the rugs ... I would greatly appreciate the continued use of these designs.[19]

Several well-known traders, including A. J. Newcomb, J. D. Foutz, and J. M. Drolet, also expressed thanks for the use of designs. Elizabeth Rorick at Shonto Trading Post, Tuba City, Arizona, wrote,

I am very much interested indeed, in what you have to say about the possibility of certain types of Navajo rugs fitting with the present new trend of decoration. For this idea has been uppermost in my mind, and I have had my weavers trying out various things with this goal in view. Principally relying on color, either pure, or in combination, together with simplicity of pattern and a lack of confusing detail. For this latter I have turned to the old patterns of years ago, before the white influence, you might say, and I believe we may come near the right feeling in this way.

But so far I have done nothing here with the vegetable dyes though in previous years I have experimented with them in my own weaving. But the shade of red to be gotten and that of the yellow from the rabbit weed, has never particularly appealed to me in the modern rug. Perhaps I am wrong, but I prefer some of the soft shades to be gotten from the proper handling and blending of the aniline dyes. Right now, I am having several of the best weavers trying to duplicate the exact shade of soft red with a yellow cast that is so beautiful in old blankets. However, if you feel that eventually I should combine the vegetable dye work with the old patterns, that would be something for me to consider. I do not want to be prejudiced, and I will be very glad to hear what you might have to say about this.[20]

Previously, many traders had encouraged the making of rugs, as distinct from blankets, and decreed that the former should have borders. Some took their ideas from commercially produced rugs right out of the Sears catalog, and envisioned the Navajos' work as competitive with this market. Moris Burge wrote to LaFarge, "Such a point has been made of borders, and I understand traders have in the past stressed the necessity for them to such an extent, that we have come to look upon them as a plague. 'Linoleum pattern' is as derogatory and accurate a term as we have been able to coin for the horrible designs they are using now."[21] Today, some of the most desirable and well-made Navajo rugs have borders. Burge and others underestimated the way innovation could revive an art or craft.

Bill Cousins, who began helping his trader father in 1915 at the age of ten, wrote in his journal about the reintroduction of vegetable dyes. While Mary Wheelwright and Lucy Cabot were working with the EAIA to find better commercial dyes for Navajo weavers, others were experimenting with the old vegetable dyes for commercial production. Cousins reveals how strongly a trader could influence a design or method through selective rewards:

> Sally and Bill Lippincott [Sallie Wagner and her husband Bill Lippincott, who ran the Wide Ruins Trading Post from 1938 to 1948] were influential in bringing in vegetable dyes . . . They didn't want rugs with manufactured wool dye . . . Well, we didn't buy many rugs. If I remember right we didn't buy any. After about six or eight months one of the better weavers brought in a vegetable dye rug. We paid through the nose for it and hung it up in the store, telling all how much we had paid for it. It didn't take long; soon Wide Ruins was noted for its rugs . . . Vegetable dye was what the weavers made up themselves—it was made from wild plants, also different barks were used, for instance the bark from the roots of a red cedar tree made a beautiful pastel red. None of the colors would scream at you. They were all a soft pastel. One of the soft reds was from lichens, a fungus that was growing on the scrub oak trees.[22]

In the late 1920s and early 1930s, Elizabeth and Martha White and other art patrons bought fine examples of Indian artwork to show at annual juried fairs in Santa Fe, sponsored by the NMAIA. (Elizabeth also acquired a large proportion of the entire 1930 and 1931 fairs for the Exposition of Indian Tribal Arts and the Ishauu shop.) By the mid-1930s the NMAIA had begun holding juried fairs at individual pueblos. Judges came from Santa Fe to view the works of the artisans, as did tourists; but the connoisseur collectors stayed away. In the late 1930s, Maria Chabot organized a fair in Santa Fe at which each pueblo was invited to show for a day dedicated to them alone. They proved successful for the artisans and evolved into today's Santa Fe Indian Market.

> These Saturday markets, for which Chabot solicited the participation of potters directly rather than through the intermediary of each pueblo's governor, represented a profound break with the past. Chabot further involved the potters by asking their help in publicizing and judging the markets. She did make a concession to Pueblo customs by assigning a specific area under the

portal [of the Palace of Governors] to a village and allowing its leaders to designate who would sit where ...

Indian Market now contains important elements of the Indian Fairs of the 1920s and the Summer Indian Market of 1936: the emphasis on prizes to point out "good" pottery for potters and buyers is a legacy from early fairs. And from the 1936 markets we have what is now taken for granted: artists representing themselves under the portal of the Palace of Governors.[23]

Elizabeth continued to push on all fronts to develop the Indian art market. Maria Chabot wrote numerous articles on Indian arts and crafts, and Hodge, artist and collector Kenneth Chapman, and others lectured on the subject across the country. The pool of Indian art authorities expanded as the organizers of this development effort realized they needed qualified judges to maintain consistent, high standards. Margretta Dietrich wrote to Elizabeth White about one such program:

At the October [1934] meeting of [the NMAIA], Mr. Meem asked if the Indian Arts Fund would give a training course for judges. As a result of that suggestion, we have just completed a course of ten lectures on Modern Indian Art at the Laboratory of Anthropology. Mr. K. M. Chapman gave four lectures ... The attendance was more than gratifying, from 60 to 90 people at each lesson; 25 signed to prepare themselves for judging. An examination is to be given in the near future to the judges class.[24]

No one—not even Elizabeth White—passed the exam developed by Kenneth Chapman. Students were asked to examine works of art and craft and answer questions about them, for example,

Weavings: How can you tell that this sample is not woven on a Chimayo loom? Which samples use twill weave? Which samples have no dye? Which sample has something distinctive in the direction of warp threads?
Pottery: Assess the purpose or functional use of the pot; the type of clay; the type of design; the defects; the decorative style.[25]

Chapman's lectures covered both objective and subjective criteria. For pottery, these included:

Firing—no smoke spots.

Condition—no scratches, rubbed spots, no defects such as scratches, blisters, cracking, popping.

Slip—complete coverage.

Form—typical of Pueblo style. Symmetric within the bounds of handmade.

Decoration—no smears, good color.

Rhythm—consistent relation and connection of parts.

Harmony—consistency of likeness, having something in common.

Unity—terms which are in interior accord.

Balance—selection of contrasts so that each part keeps place within a whole.[26]

Chapman's sense that Indian traditions were rapidly disappearing lent an urgency to the matter of preserving and revitalizing Indian arts and crafts. "It is my hope," he wrote, "that coming generations of our people will find [the Indians] still holding to the best of the old culture and making it possible for

Artist and Pueblo pottery expert Kenneth Chapman, ca. 1915.

America to draw continued inspiration from them."[27] Chapman and others encouraged an aesthetic based on the best work of the classical period—from the 1500s to about 1880. One manifestation of this was the effort to establish standards of "genuineness."

In 1932 Elizabeth joined the United Indian Traders Association (UITA), organized by traders to deal with the threat of "handmade" Indian goods coming from commercial producers. At the time, Maisel Indian Traders in Albuquerque was mass-producing imitations of the finest work done by Navajo silversmiths on the reservation. The UITA celebrated a victory in 1933 when the Federal Trade Commission ordered Maisel to stop labeling machine-made jewelry as Indian or Indian made. J. L. Ambrose, a trader in Thoreau, New Mexico, wrote to Elizabeth, "Our Navajos are happy to learn of the decision, and we have great hopes of employing many more silversmiths in the future, also, we shall be able to pay our smiths more for their work."[28]

The UITA experimented with the practice of using a government stamp for genuine Indian handmade products. The standards were rigorous. Elizabeth described them in a letter of 19 January 1932, in response to an inquiry:

My dear Miss Kissell:

The standards set up by the United Indian Traders Association are as follows:

Indian Handmade Blankets or Rugs: Material used shall be virgin wool or virgin angora wool, hand-washed, hand-carded, and hand-dyed, the warp shall be all wool and hand-spun, the woof shall be all wool and hand-spun and the blanket or rug shall be hand-woven by an Indian.

Indian Handmade Pottery: Shall be of native clay, handmixed, handshaped not using a wheel, hand-painted, the paint shall be handmade and the decorations shall be put on by hand, it shall be fired in the manner in which the Indians were accustomed to doing before the coming of the whiteman.

Indian Handmade Basketry: The material for the baskets shall be raised on or adjacent to the reservation where the baskets are made, the dyes handmade and the basket hand-woven by the Indians themselves in the manner in which they were accustomed to doing in the early days.

Indian Handmade and Hand-Hammered Silverware: The silver used in making Indian silverware should be 950 fine as used in the good old diez pesos; if diez pesos are not used the quality and size of the discs or squares should be the same as in the old diez pesos, which is one ounce in size, 950 fine; if an article requires more than one peso or one ounce, then they should be melted together and hand-hammered by the Indian; all Indian silver-craft that is eligible [for] a Government guarantee tag should be hand-hammered by the Indian; the decoration should be put on with dies that are hand-made by the Indian and all semi-precious stones used for decoration should be genuine and not imitation.[29]

Ultimately, this practice was discontinued because of the difficulty of agreeing on standards and administering the stamp fairly.

The Indian Market, the Indian Arts Fund's educational role, design and dyes projects—these combined efforts gave the Southwest Association on Indian Affairs (SWAIA, the descendant of the NMAIA) a commanding position in regard to Indian arts and crafts in the Southwest. Today the annual Santa Fe Indian Market, sponsored by SWAIA, is the premier marketing event in the world for American Indian arts and crafts.

In the mid-1930s Elizabeth White's former friend, Elizabeth Shepley Sergeant, was hired by John Collier as a research worker in community studies. In a report titled "Notes on a Changing Culture, As Affected by Indian Art," Sergeant analyzed some of the consequences of the new popularity of Indian paintings:

The student of cultural transformations finds rich food at the Pueblo of San Ildefonso which has, for a quarter of a century, been a special nursling of lovers of Indian arts and crafts. Its gifts and accessibility to Santa Fe have brought about that leading San Ildefonso craftsmen—or artists, if you prefer— are known by name and in person to leading white authorities, artists, traders, and to many plain citizens of the town. The San Ildefonso Indians have made a contact with white life unique so far among the Pueblos. This has brought them both gain and loss.

Top, the First Southwest Indian Fair, held in Santa Fe in 1922, was an early precursor of today's Indian Market; left, Elizabeth White gave this Navajo late Classic blanket, ca. 1860–65, to the IAF in 1931.

The gain is clear; it has given these Indians—at least the most fortunate among them—better homes and food. It has given a number of them auto-mobiles, to replace the slow-going wagon. It has given them, in the social sense, ease in the white world, and ability to stand on their own feet, through the recognized validity of craft techniques.

The loss is less clear—at least the casual white observer fails to recognize it. Indeed San Ildefonso is often vaunted as a highly "traditional" Pueblo group because it paints and dances and makes fine pottery—"Old Pueblo characteristics."

But this is an aesthetic valuation. When spiritual and religious values are transformed into material or aesthetic values, something vital and basic in Indian life has come to an end. [30]

Then Sergeant discussed the sources of cultural change:

In studying the history of the transformation, the catalysers of the change from the old agricultural economy—the corn, wheat, alfalfa pattern, as we know it at Zia or Domingo—from which grew pottery painting and ritual—seem to be three.

First, the leadership and interest of certain white Indian scientists in Santa Fe; Hewett and Chapman undoubtedly built the bridge over which the Indian could travel to a new type of life and livelihood.

Second, the inherent and unusual gifts of the San Ildefonso Indians for design, painting and modeling clay.

Third—and not least important—the acute need and desire for money and greater ease on the part of a proud Pueblo group, land poor and water poor, for generations and at the time of the shift to a new economy took place—declining in population.

The pressure of these factors probably produced in 1921, that inner explosion of energy which led to the invention of a new pottery type and then its home manufacture on quite new terms for pueblo life …[Here she refers to the black-on-black pottery developed by Maria Martinez and her family].

As the "Old Pueblo" wall began to show breaches where fine ancestral pots could go out, and milled flour enter, spiritual factors, political factors, created more breakdowns in the ancient customs. Even among the Pueblos, a Renaissance was preceded by a war. The Bursum Bill threatened Indian rights and customs but raised an army of white sympathizers and defenders for the support of the Pueblo Indian—including his arts and ceremonies. So these ceremonies were more attended—because more advertised. It is probable that but for the Indian Arts Fund, the Indian Fairs, [and] all attempts of the early 1920's for the conservation of Indian values in New Mexico, not by Indian but by whites, there would be no Laboratory of Anthropology. The San Ildefonso ceramic treasures have been "preserved" by these means—again more for and by whites than for Indians.

Sergeant identified efforts that fostered these changes, specifically mentioning Elizabeth White's contributions:

The New York market for Indian art came into being as a "smart market" because Miss A. E. White, on an altruistic basis, and at a loss in money, started her Madison Avenue Shop. So [a painter] could earn $30.00 for a painting and thus could desert farming to earn $900 in one year. These things form an endless chain of cause and effect—good in the sense that they enlarged the opportunity of the San Ildefonso Indian, but none the less, causing deep and subtle changes in his way of life, such changes as even an Indian in the end had to recognize and rationalize.

Margaret McKittrick Burge was already giving what today would be called "technical advice" regarding the marketing and production of Indian arts and crafts. Speaking to an Indian Service conference of home economics teachers at Fort Wingate, New Mexico, in August 1934, she said:

Generally speaking, all handcraft falls into two broad classifications, competitive and non-competitive; that is, articles which compete in the open market with machine made articles of similar type, and those which have no machine competition.

The inevitable unfortunate fate of the handcraft which enters the competitive field is . . . forcibly driven home when the state of the silver craft is

Navajo silver necklace donated by Elizabeth White to the IAF in 1945.

considered . . . Originally, hand-wrought Navajo silver commanded a good price and sold quite well. Unfortunately, the white man found it would pay to imitate it with machine goods. These machine-made imitations also sold well but in a cheaper market than the hand-wrought articles. Then a fatal mistake was made. Instead of concentrating on holding the luxury market, turning out finer, more expensive, heavier hand-wrought pieces which could not be imitated by machine, thereby keeping Navajo silver in a non-competitive class, the hand workers of silver attempted to enter into direct competition with the machine-made goods. Wherever possible, machines, torches, drawplates, machine dies, etc. were introduced into the hogans. Silversmiths were forced to turn out dozens and dozens of identical rings or bracelets, prices to the workers and to the dealers dropped lower and lower, the machine made products continued to flood the market. As far as I know, Navajo silver within the authentic tradition of Navajo design is now made only in two or three localities on the entire Reservation and at the Santa Fe Indian School.

What is the quality that gives value to handcraft? It has no name and it is difficult to define. But it is the quality that makes a Navajo rug or bracelet, or a Pueblo jar different from any other rug or bracelet or jar in the world. It is an intrinsic and inherent quality that comes from the particular material used, the handling of the materials, the exclusive, non-imitative design.[31]

While in Spain for the 1929 Seville Exposition, Elizabeth made a side trip to Morocco in order to investigate the French government's efforts to support Moroccan handicrafts. Convinced that the US government should also play a part in encouraging handicrafts, she, Percy Jackson, and other members of the EAIA proposed an Indian Arts and Crafts Board to Indian Commissioner Burke and his successor, Charles Rhoads. Rhoads was more sympathetic, but neither man was inclined to back the idea.

Traders and advocates both played key roles in mediating between modern American culture and the cultures of the Southwest Indians in the 1930s. Ultimately, the Indians would mediate for themselves, but this transition was not to come until after World War II. Meanwhile, Elizabeth White and her colleagues proposed, needled, inspired, and competed with John Collier to come up with a government-sponsored Indian Arts and Crafts Board to support the work in an institutional framework.

Guests celebrating the opening of El Delirio's new swimming pool, ca. 1926.

A Circle of Friends

Elizabeth White's love for indigenous folk arts may have kindled her enthusiasm for the young and romantic profession of anthropology. Among her anthropologist friends White discovered an approach to life that reflected her own, one that sought out the deeper connections between people.

When she visited Sylvanus Morley and Herbert Spinden in Guatemala in 1914, she took a steamer and then proceeded on muleback to the archaeological sites, including that at Quirigua. During these early years Morley and Spinden were making fantastic discoveries. Reports came north:

> Sylvanus Morley, the brilliant young Harvard scientist of Santa Fe, now at work in the effort to tear aside the veil of mystery which shrouds the ancient monuments of prehistoric peoples in Central America, has made a number of discoveries recently which have set the scientific world by the ears.
>
> Word has just come from the heart of the jungle of British Honduras that Morley has discovered no less than eight new "initial series" in deciphering the dates of the monuments of the Mayas.[1]

Morley, Spinden, and their colleagues were pioneering new methods of archaeological excavation and historic preservation. Elizabeth White provided financial support for a number of Morley's digs and other archaeological ventures in Central America. Morley, in turn, tutored her in anthropological matters, attended many of her parties, and delivered at least one illustrated lecture at El Delirio about his work at the Temple of the Two Lintels at Chichén Itza.

Herbert Joseph Spinden, known to his friends as Joe, was "an affable, dedicated man" who at one time wanted to marry Elizabeth, according to William White Howells.[2] Spinden had "a mind which sought the relations among disparate data" and "boldly fused the results of his study with a high sense of values to examine his own contemporary culture."[3] He deplored the government's treatment of Indians and dedicated much of his energy to correcting the balance.

Elizabeth White agreed with this vision, as evidenced most clearly in her support of fine craftsmanship and her work on behalf of Indian health. But she diverged from Spinden's advocacy of artisanship as an antidote to modern business and government economic policies and his sense that these policies failed to preserve and vitalize the cultural "oversoul." She was very much a part of the business world in holding and managing her investments as she did. At the same time she carried the mantle of philanthropy in counterbalance to the aggressive side of business life, and she contributed to the possibilities for Indian artisans to carry on this ideal in the modern world.

When the John D. Rockefeller–funded Laboratory of Anthropology was established in Santa Fe in 1927, the White sisters donated fifty acres from the De Vargas Development to the new institution. Elizabeth was elected to the board of directors and served on its executive committee from 1927 to 1933. A virtual Who's Who of American anthropology, the board also included the Lab's first director, Jesse Nusbaum; Edgar Lee Hewett, director of the School of American Research and the Museum of New Mexico; Kenneth M. Chapman of the School of American Research; Ralph Linton of the Field Museum of Natural History; A. L. Kroeber, University of California; Franz Boas, Columbia University; Alfred V. Kidder, Phillips Academy; Neil Judd, Smithsonian Institution; F. W. Hodge, Museum of the American Indian; Clark Wissler, American

Top, archaeologist Sylvanus Morley at Quirigua, Guatemala, in 1911; bottom, Elizabeth White and anthropologists at the Laboratory of Anthropology, Santa Fe, ca. 1930.

Museum of Natural History; Sylvanus Morley, Carnegie Institution of Washington; Elsie Clews Parsons, Southwest Society; and Bronson M. Cutting, US Senator from New Mexico. Jesse Nusbaum wrote to Elizabeth, "I have had several good talks with Margaret McKittrick and know of her interest in all features of the work with the Indians. Her plan of bringing Indian pupils to our collections is admirable and you may rest assured . . . the most is made of these opportunities."[4]

Elizabeth was also a founding member of the Indian Arts Fund (IAF), established in Santa Fe in 1922 for the purpose of collecting, preserving, and making available for study fine Indian works of the period from roughly 1600 to 1880. Both she and Martha served on the IAF board.

In the 1930s Elizabeth helped her friend and EAIA associate, Mary Cabot Wheelwright, fulfill her dream of establishing a living museum that would embody the spirit of the hogan, the traditional rounded Navajo home in which most Navajo ceremonies were conducted. Wheelwright's vision was described in a 1931 proposal to the Laboratory of Anthropology. William Penhallow Henderson, the artist who had designed El Delirio, came up with a plan for a large structure shaped like a traditional hogan. It would serve

> not as a mere housing for a collection but as an exhibit itself, inside and out. Its purpose is to perpetuate the spirit of the Navajo "hogan" not as an exact replica, but on a scale in keeping with that spirit . . . It is difficult to think of sand-paintings without the hogan—just as it is impossible to think of a Catholic mass without the Cathedral.
>
> Symbolically, a medicine "hogan" represents the emergence of man—from non-living to life. You may take this symbolism on any plane you choose—from the underworld to this, from the womb to birth, from a lower state of consciousness to a higher.[4]

The proposal went on to describe the entrance to the museum as symbolic of a spiritual passage.

During the development process, Mary Wheelwright wrote to Kidder, explaining her work among the Navajo and the purpose of the museum. She described the basic elements of Navajo religion she wished to incorporate and

Interior of the newly constructed Wheelwright Museum in the 1930s.

concluded, "My idea for this building and collection is not ... That it be a place for the collection of one person or from one medicine man ... but a depository in a beautiful form for the most remarkable primitive religion that I have ever studied."[6]

Several members of the Laboratory of Anthropology board objected to the hogan design. Francis I. Proctor, the Boston eye specialist who spent his summers doing volunteer work for Indian public health, wrote to Elizabeth White, "The truth is that the plans submitted represent an artistic interpretation and are not the real thing at all. Now I feel that in a scientific institution everything should be founded on the truth. If we are to have a hogan, it should be a *real* hogan and not an attempt at some mystical, occult interpretation."[7]

Sylvanus Morley opposed the inclusion of a skylight in the design. Regarding the stipulation that the museum have an eastern entrance, as hogans do, he maintained, "The topography really requires entrance from the north or west."[8] This was a situation in which artistic vision was in conflict with scientific rigor. Poet Alice Corbin Henderson wrote to Elizabeth, "The Committee is, I think, frankly *scared,* because the Hogan is unique and different. Though this is just what would make it an asset. But they have no architectural imagination and no courage."[9]

Eventually Elizabeth White simply gave the Wheelwright Museum a separate piece of land so that it could exist as Mary Wheelwright envisioned it. Elizabeth was able to grasp the import of an idea in a way the archaeologists could not. Although she respected their scientific vision, she did not let it get in the way of a larger sense of how life, art, and science interweave in ways that can be appreciated through imagination. Elizabeth recognized that a spirit of life could be honored as easily by an imaginative architectural design as by a "real" hogan, and perhaps better.

If friendship is the measure of a life, Elizabeth's and Martha's cups were full during their years together in Santa Fe, up to Martha's death in 1937. The social set at El Delirio included Percy and Alice Jackson, Jack Lambert, William Penhallow and Alice Corbin Henderson, Witter Bynner, John and Dolly Sloan, Gus and Jane Baumann, Randall and Belle Davey, J. B. Jackson, and Henry and Kay Hoyt. And they welcomed into the heart of their household their butler, Knut Goxem.

It was Percy and Alice Day Jackson who introduced Elizabeth to New Mexico in 1913. Percy was a New York lawyer who handled organizational matters for the EAIA. Alice, who had been at Bryn Mawr with Elizabeth, was an avid art aficionada. It may have been she who inspired and guided Elizabeth's interest in art as a way to help Southwestern Indians achieve self-sufficiency.

New York painter John Sloan and his wife, Dolly, were frequent visitors to Santa Fe and El Delirio. Sloan recalled,

> Out in Santa Fe I enjoyed seeing artist friends like Will Shuster and Joe Bakos. We all spent many evenings together just talking and having a few drinks. It was a relaxation from the months of work in New York. Then we artists and some of the writers like Witter Bynner helped to revive the old Spanish Historical Parade to celebrate the re-entry of De Vargas into the city back in 1685 *[sic]*. Dolly Sloan used to collect money for the annual fiesta event. Then we put on the Hysterical Parade for fun. I used to spend hours working on floats and costumes. It reminded me of the Philadelphia days when we newspapermen used to put on amateur theatricals.

One trouble with Santa Fe was that there was too much social life. You could get caught up with too many late nights out.[10]

In 1932 Sloan gave a series of four talks on art at El Delirio in which he put forth his philosophy: "Good drawing is the ability to put down a graphic or plastic intention of the mind, not the ability to put down, or repeat, or reflect a visual sensation."[11] "Art is the response of the living to life," he would write later in *The Gist of Art*. This viewpoint was shared to some degree by Elizabeth, who collected many traditional works of folk art and watercolors with great human feeling in them as distinct from those that were merely charming or decorative. According to Sloan's biographer, Van Wyck Brooks,

> Sloan was enthralled by the Indians and their dances and art, partly because he had recently awakened to a sense of the value of tradition and a deeper sense of the problems of aesthetic form. The Indians, he saw at once, had a great traditional base and worked together like the unknown artists who were inspired by a communal feeling in Gothic times, but the idea of such a thing had previously been abstract with him—he had never encountered a living aesthetic tradition.[12]

Sloan painted Elizabeth's portrait in 1934 and later wrote, "My sitter asserts her liking for this picture which to my mind rates her high in ability to look on a picture as a created work."[13] There is an almost dour quality to Elizabeth's expression. Catherine Rayne later asked Sloan, "What was on your mind when you did that awful portrait of Miss E.? You made her look as if she had driven her car over a bunch of children." He responded, "Well, I wasn't going to have anyone think I was beholden to her." The painting shows a strong-willed, almost hard woman. What it left out was the grace that ameliorated that strength.

Dolly, Sloan's first wife, was a close associate of Elizabeth. She contributed her time to the National Association on Indian Affairs, which operated out of Elizabeth's New York shop and gallery. She also managed the transfer of Elizabeth's art treasures from the gallery to museums and schools after Martha died. Elizabeth, devastated by her sister's death, relied heavily on Dolly Sloan's judgment and practical execution of this enormous task.

Clockwise from top left: John and Dolly Sloan, 1932; portrait of Elizabeth White by John Sloan, 1934; Witter Bynner with two Pueblo Indian friends, 1922; Jane and Gustave Baumann, with Punch, on their front porch in Santa Fe, 1925.

El Delirio's estate manager, Jack Lambert, on Tom Thumb (left) and Eldon Butler on Buck.

If John Sloan matched Elizabeth in his classicist approach to matters of art, Gustave Baumann matched her broad renaissance taste as the embodiment of a master craftsman and artist. Baumann's distinctive color woodcut prints have made him one of the most popular Southwest landscape artists of the century. His wife, Jane Henderson Baumann, was an opera singer who had moved to New Mexico to study Indian music.

Jack Lambert was a friend to the Whites from the time they established themselves in Santa Fe to the end of Elizabeth's life, serving as their estate manager, tour guide, and builder. A cowboy who held real respect for his Indian counterparts, he was an important link between Elizabeth and groups of Plains Indians. Lambert knew some of the members of the Shoshone tribe, from whom he acquired several examples of fine arts and crafts for Elizabeth's collections and shop. The New Mexico State Archives holds film footage of a trip Lambert and the White sisters took to Rainbow Bridge in Utah in the late 1920s or early 1930s. A woman recognizable as Elizabeth by her hat and walk is climbing a steep sandstone rock. Lambert is at the top of the rock, pulling in the rope tied around her waist as she climbs. Another clip shows Lambert in a fancy pair of chaps, decorated with a swirl of embroidered designs, riding a horse on the White sisters' land.

Still another film clip is of a mule picking up a block with a number on it and carrying it to the other end of the corral. The mule's name was Paloma. "Paloma was better at math than I was," said Marjorie (Marge) Lambert, an archaeologist who married Jack in 1950.[14] The local newspaper reported Paloma's accomplishments:

INTELLECTUAL ASS—LA PALOMA, MULE OF MENTALITY,
COUNTS, SPELLS, RECLINES AT WHITE TEA PARTY

La Paloma is a marvelous mule. Apparently lacking the mulishness of most
mules, of attractive form and feature, with a winning countenance and affectionate disposition, La Paloma, property of the Misses Martha and Elizabeth
White, performed admirably at a tea party at the White hacienda yesterday
under the direction of Jack Lambert. Responsive to Jack's suggestion, La
Paloma picked out blocks with numbers on them as requested and brought
them to Lambert. Likewise she picked out three blocks in orthoepical
sequence to spell the appropriate word, "Tea."[15]

Lambert and the Whites often visited the Rio Grande pueblos, where they enjoyed the ceremonial dances. He took them to Zuni several times, to Hopi country, and on a pack trip to the Navajo Reservation. A photo shows Elizabeth, Lambert, and another person in front of a 1920s model Lincoln stuck in a wash, the waters of a flash flood sweeping past them. Elizabeth's pants legs are rolled up and she is wading through knee-deep water to shore. An article in the paper noted, "The Misses White had attended the buffalo dance at Cochiti and started to follow other cars across the Santa Fe wash, with Jack Lambert at the wheel. The hind wheels went down rather ominously and at the suggestion of the driver the party got out and waded ashore in knee-deep water just as the brown current got about two inches deep in the tonneau. When they reached shore the water was half way up the side curtains."[16]

Lambert and the Whites got along, in part, because of their shared inter-ests, such as Indian life and books. He was courteous, thoughtful, and compe-tent, qualities that appealed to the Whites, while their insistence on quality and thoroughness undoubtedly appealed to him. "He was the last of the Western gentlemen," said Evelyn Measles, who knew Lambert for thirty years."[17] He was also a spirited man. During one of their pack trips, Elizabeth overheard Eldon Butler ask Jack, "Do you think this coffee is strong enough?" Jack answered, "Throw a nail in it and if it floats, it's strong enough."[18]

Before moving to Santa Fe with her husband, artist and architect William Penhallow Henderson, Alice Corbin Henderson was a well-known poet and co-editor of the avant-garde Chicago-based magazine, *Poetry*. Like El Delirio, the Hendersons' Santa Fe home became a meeting place for the local artistic and literary community, and Alice worked with Elizabeth White to fight the Bursum Bill and to market Indian arts and crafts. Poet Witter Bynner was another regular guest at the White parties and a collaborator on the Exposition of Indian Tribal Arts. He and Elizabeth shared an interest in the Orient—she had visited Japan as a young woman, he had lived for a period in China.

Knut Goxem, the butler at El Delirio from 1923 to 1959, was "a thin, Winston Churchill-like character, only not as jowly. He was semi-bald, ruddy, with a nice round face. He always wore a suit . . . He was a friendly man, informal in a formal way."[19] When a gregarious guest grabbed his hand and introduced himself, Goxem responded, "Sir, I am a servant." The guest returned, "Hell, man, I'm Bob! I want to shake your hand."

*El Delirio's butler,
Knut Goxem.*

Once Goxem was serving at a dinner party Elizabeth gave for her cousin Norval Richardson, the US ambassador to Italy. The subject of conversation at the table was Lady Godiva's nude ride for charity, which had been recently recreated in New York. None of the guests could remember whose music had accompanied the ride. Goxem bent down to Elizabeth as he served and whispered, "Saint-Saëns, madam." On another occasion, when Goxem was going out for the evening, Elizabeth decided to make dinner for her guests. Catherine Rayne remembers, "Knut returned later and found us piling the dishes in the sink. 'Get away from my sink,' he yelled. 'That Crown Derby goes in one plate at a time!' "

There was a gaiety, an exuberance, and an innocence among the people who gathered at El Delirio. Santa Fe writer Pen LaFarge, whose father, writer Oliver LaFarge, was a part of this social scene, said, "They could enjoy the ferment of the times without the lost feeling of the Paris group of American expatriates."[20]

When the White sisters built the first swimming pool in Santa Fe, they celebrated its completion with a play written for the occasion by poet Witter Bynner, in which King Chac Xib Chac dedicated the ceremonial pool to the Great Feathered Serpent and prayed for rain—and one other blessing:

> But I, his Herald, have been told,
> Because His Majesty is suffering from a royal cold,
> That I may lift my voice this day in a cadenza
> And beg the gods to lift his influenza.

Sylvanus Morley, the renowned Mayan explorer and archaeologist, played one of the characters in this take-off on Mayan ceremony. Other players included Bynner, Alice Henderson, Percy Jackson, and former New Mexico governor Herbert Hagerman. The occasion was memorialized by Gustave Baumann in his map of El Delirio.

Martha and Elizabeth had been enthusiastic thespians ever since childhood; one of Elizabeth's earliest memories was of playing pioneers and Indians with her sisters. Bryn Mawr College encouraged this predilection by providing ample opportunity for theater, including the elaborate May Day pageants they

Top, members of the audience enjoying the mock Mayan ceremony for the new swimming pool, ca. 1926; bottom, swimmers enjoying the pool.

Top, scenes from Martha's play El Baile de la Rifa, *1931: left, Norman McGee, Martha Root White, and Juan Sedillo; right, Spanish dancers. Bottom, the Whites' contingent in Santa Fe Fiesta parade in front of the Scottish Rite Temple, ca. 1934.*

The Pietro Longhi party, ca. 1953. Elizabeth (left) and Catherine together; musicians play in the choir loft of the living room; refreshments were served in the dining room.

both found parts in. The sisters' Santa Fe parties were often occasions for theater, with guests dressed up in costume according to a chosen theme. One example was the 1931 performance of *El Baile de la Rifa*, a play written by Martha and set in Andalusia, Spain. The cast—Martha White, Elizabeth White, Jane Baumann, Witter Bynner, Will Shuster, Dr. Harry Mera, Dorothy Stewart, John Gaw Meem, Leonora Curtin, and William P. Henderson, among others—included many of the social, artistic, and political leaders of Santa Fe in the 1920s and 1930s.

Many of the same people were on hand for other lavish El Delirio occasions such as the Pietro Longhi party (named after the eighteenth-century Italian painter) held in the garden and the chapel. Musicians in the balcony play what one imagines was Mexican folk music, though it could just as easily have been big-band music. The guests are costumed as if for a masked ball. Balloons hang from the vigas above two great Mexican tin chandeliers.

Guests at a Santa Fe Fiesta party at El Delirio in the mid-1930s included artists Will Schuster and Randall Davey, Jane Baumann, dancer Jacques Cartier and his companion, Ray Baldwin, Mary Morley, wife of archaeologist Sylvanus Morley, and John and Dolly Sloan. The local paper reported:

> Thanks to the rains here and in the southern part of the state a party that is sure to be the most original of the Fiesta season was held last night to the delight of several hundreds of guests in the chapel at the White hacienda.
>
> Practically everything happened just before time for the party at 8:30 o'clock that might have spoiled the evening. Word was received that the Mariachis who were to play would not arrive until today being held up by floods in El Paso. The sudden down-pour of rain about 3 o'clock soaked the out-door setting which was planned and forced a last minute change from the arroyo into the chapel. The luminarias were too wet to be lighted.
>
> But Miss Martha and Miss Amelia Elizabeth White were ready when their guests arrived to put on the nicest kind of entertainment. With a large group of friends assisting, the impromptu program was something that is seldom duplicated in a large gathering.
>
> Everyone with a stunt to contribute took part. In addition, Los Villeros Alegres played during the program and for dancing afterward.

Elizabeth in Santa Fe Fiesta costume, ca. 1932.

Starting the program off professionally were Jacques Cartier, the New York dancer that Santa Fe has so taken to heart, and Mary Morley, his piano accompanist. Cartier danced several Spanish numbers including the favorite from Granada and one not danced here before this summer. Later he returned in full Indian regalia to dance the mescale dance of the Hopi Indians to the beat of the tom-tom held by Ray Baldwin.

In the meantime there was John Sloan with his uproarious pantomimes, the one in a restaurant, another on a 5th Ave. bus ...Will Shuster was on hand to do his professional "flea" act for which he was elegantly whiskered . . . Randall Davey brought down the house with his recitations ...

Miss Morley returned to accompany Jane Baumann in her song interpretations so beloved of Santa Fe, and Mrs. Baumann led the cheering as Miss Morley played and sang one of her own melodious compositions. Mrs. Baumann's "Bird in a Gilded Cage" was the first part of her act, then came all of her graceful, delightful nonsense, with full change of costume executed behind a door. There was "Home Sur Le Range" in grand opera style and wonderful French accent; an improvised Indian song and dance with Cartier, as an encore to the touristic "Land of Sky Blue Water" for which he picked at the tiny drum while she sang.

Two "old santos" were a living picture act by Dolly Sloan and Jane Baumann in sheets and make-up ... John Sloan led the singing of "Rolling Home" to wind up the evening of home talent fun. Mr. Davey played the guitar for this.

Nearly all of the guests were costumed for this first Fiesta party, as were the hostesses.[21]

At El Delirio, Elizabeth and Martha established the Rathmullan Kennels to raise Irish wolfhounds and Afghan hounds. (The former kennel building now houses the SAR Press and the SAR Archaeology program.) They hired Alex Scott, a professional trainer, to work with the dogs and take them to shows throughout the country, where they won dozens of championship prizes. The kennel operation was described in the May 1934 issue of *The American Kennel Gazette*:

> The health of the Rathmullan dogs is watched very closely ... The rooms are washed out completely and disinfected ... Three times a week. The runs are moistened with a hose every day, and sprayed with sheep dip, twice a week ... The morning meal is very light, consisting of two handfuls of Peerless Ration, one egg, and half a pint of milk, per dog. In Winter, a tablespoon of cod-liver oil is added, for each dog.
>
> The evening meal is the main one, of course. On four days of the week, each hound gets at least 3 and 1/2 lbs. of raw, lean beef ... The three other evenings, they have cooked meat, along with carrots, spinach, and onions, thickened with Ration or biscuit. On occasional days, they have fish, instead of meat.[22]

This complicated diet was the primary reason Elizabeth eventually stopped raising dogs during World War II, when beef was difficult to obtain. (The diet was also a source of local conflict, for rumor had it that the dogs were being fed milk in a time of milk rationing.) For a brief period Elizabeth was the regional director of Dogs for Defense, and the kennel was used to train various dogs for the war effort.

Top, Rathmullan Kennels manager Alec Scott and Irish wolfhounds, ca. 1933; bottom, Elizabeth (left) and Martha with their Irish wolfhounds Balbricken, Edain, Gareth, and Sagramohr, ca. 1933.

In 1939 Elizabeth gave an animal shelter to the City of Santa Fe in memory of Martha and her love of animals. After Alex Scott died in 1957, Elizabeth decreed that her own dogs were to live out their lives on the estate. They were buried in a cemetery across the arroyo from the kennels, near Elizabeth's and Martha's final resting place. The dogs' graves are marked by individual wooden crosses.

Martha (second from left), Elizabeth (with wolfhounds), and friends, in 16th-century English hunting costume for the Santa Fe Fiesta parade, ca. 1933.

Martha Root White was only 57 when she died of cancer in 1937. Until then, the White household had had the feel of a grand Italian spectacle. From dog shows at St. Michael's College and horse shows at the Breese Ranch on Upper Canyon Road to Santa Fe Fiesta parties, Elizabeth's and Martha's lives were full of pageantry.

It is not known when Martha learned that she had cancer. As a Christian Scientist she apparently chose not to pursue available medical treatments, though she and Elizabeth visited the hot springs in Bath, England, in 1936. It is also hard to know whether the spectacular aspect of their lives was driven by their awareness of Martha's disease, but that would not have been out of character for these two who delighted in a good play and a good party.

Martha was a strong influence on her sister's life. Although younger by two years, she had always been the instigator, and her greater physical size and gregariousness contrasted with Elizabeth's tiny body and more reserved nature. "Unlike Ish, who was small and stylish, Martha had her coloratura and stature," remembered William White Howells.[23]

This contrast held true from early on, as revealed in a 1905 poem written by a family friend about a party the sisters attended in Paris:

The next to appear
Upon the scene
Was a Mr. Schmidt,
Very lank and lean.

…His roving eyes
Saw Martha White
And his spirits began
To ascend like a kite…

What did she do
This Martha White?
She talked to this man!!!
Do you think it was right?

In the meantime her sister
Was looking around,
Now coyly at the ceiling
And then at the ground,

And sure did a man
Fall to her wiles…
And devoted himself
To the little White flower.[24]

Martha Root White,
ca. 1910.

Martha could be hearty and earthy, but she was also, like her more cere-
bral sister, a woman of sensitivity. She had a lyric gift, an eye for detail, and a
knack for capturing a meaningful image, as seen in her diary description of a
1914 trip to Ireland. The Whites visited several castles, including Castle Hyde
and Rathmullan, the name they later gave to their kennels in Santa Fe:

> Castle Hyde is a perfect…house run by Miss Magill. Peacocks on lawn. Black
> water flows past, only about 50 yards away. Masses of flowers, beautifully
> arranged. Run like a private home. Afternoon tea always ready. Places
> designed at one large table for dinner, etc. Details of mouldings etc. very
> beautiful, the riser of each stair in the graceful curved stone stairway has its
> mouldings [here she made a sketch]. The ceiling edged with elaborate and
> graceful cornices.[25]

This passage calls to mind the fine quality of work that went into El Delirio.
While Elizabeth had a thorough overview, Martha's eye for detail brought
much to the estate.

*The gazebo at
El Delirio, with
François Tonetti's
bust of Martha.*

One unorthodox aspect of Martha's character was her conversion to Christian Science, which holds that mind is the central organizing principle and that the mind is God. As this principle extends into healing, it means that sickness and health are primarily spiritual rather than physical matters. Right beliefs and implacable faith are the pathways to healing. This spirit-based philosophy has more than a little in common with the healing principles of the Indians of the Southwest. The Navajo sings are, in part, rites to bring a patient back into harmony with the ordering principles of life.

Soon after Martha died, Elizabeth donated the entire collection of the Gallery of American Indian Art, amounting to approximately 1,350 pieces, to museums and schools across the country.[26] According to one newspaper report, "The collection, begun in 1912, had reached vast proportions, Miss White said in a recent interview. She had no suitable place to house it, and, besides, the basic purpose of making the collection was that of 'stimulating and supporting Indian artists by creating a wider interest and more intelligent appreciation of their work.' "[27] Elizabeth subsequently withdrew from the public eye for several years. Martha, the playwright, the daring rider who could fall off her horse going over a jump and get right back on, was gone.

Martha was cremated, and her ashes later were placed in a niche in the gazebo at El Delirio. Eventually Elizabeth would be buried, Martha's ashes interred with her, in front of the gazebo. The renowned sculptor François Tonetti, commissioned to do a relief for the New York City Public Library, used Martha's head as a model for the central muse and sent a cast of it to Elizabeth. She had the head recast in stone and set into the outer wall of the gazebo, where it looks down today on the sisters' grave.

Elizabeth in Petra, Jordan, ca. 1955.

CHAPTER 6

Further Adventures

Elizabeth White returned to the world from her extended period of mourning only after she met Catherine Rayne in the fall of 1942. Elizabeth was experiencing a severe episode of hyperthyroidism at the time, and Catherine, a nurse, was asked to attend to her. Catherine remembers,

> In October 1942 there may have been seven private-duty nurses in Santa Fe—no more and possibly less. Often there was only a day or two of leisure time between cases. I was caught up in this mad whirl for nine months. A little boy in an iron lung was followed by a woman with septicemia who was followed by another with a gall bladder removal.
>
> Desperately trying to catch a breath after the last case, I accepted an invitation from a friend who lived in the country to come out, relax, picnic, and help myself to apples from the orchard. That October 24th was a heavenly day. Then at 11 pm I was awakened by the phone from a just-attained sound sleep. Would I go on a case in the hospital? A very important benefactress of Santa Fe. Sorry. I must have some time off.

Left, Catherine Rayne, ca. 1935; right, Catherine (right) and fellow nurse,
Brun's Army Hospital, Santa Fe, ca. 1943.

1 a.m.: Please, won't you come on with Miss Amelia Elizabeth White? You know—she has the gallery on Garcia St. Sorry. You must find someone else. 3 a.m.: Miss White has the kennels on Garcia St. where she raises those stately Afghan hounds. I was not interested in Miss White's dogs.

By this time I decided I wasn't getting much sleep because of the constant importuning and I promised to go for one day while they found a permanent replacement. That one day stretched into a thirty-year association with a truly remarkable person and devoted friend.

Catherine was with the Red Cross at the time and knew that eventually she would be called for active war duty, but Elizabeth did her best to keep her at El Delirio. The commanding general of Brun's Army Hospital in Santa Fe met with Elizabeth periodically to discuss a tree-planting project. "He would come up to visit her and ask, 'How about that tree? How long did that one take to grow to this height?' She would answer, 'Oh, I don't know, I think we planted that one on such and such a date' and then turn the conversation: 'Wouldn't it be nice if Miss Rayne could be stationed at Brun's in Santa Fe?' The general would reply that he'd see what he could do, then ask about another tree."

Catherine was finally called to overseas duty in 1943. Her letters to Elizabeth described life in tents and apartments in Normandy and on leave to visit sites in Europe. (Specific locations were left out, to save the censor the trouble.) The letters display the combination of sensitivity and protective affection that would characterize Catherine's long relationship with Elizabeth.

France, 1 Dec. '44

Dear Miss White,

I must tell you of our new home. We have moved across the road from the pasture and into tents for three or four. Ours is three—Miss Frish, one of our dietitians, and I. We have cement floors, electricity, and a chunk stove besides our beautiful packing box furniture. They seem to have only one color of paint, that being bright red. It gives a rather startling effect but we shall tone that down a bit.

I have a German ammunition box the same color, that makes a very nice Christmas Chest. All in all we are quite comfortable. We have finally been issued clothing to fit the occasion and some of it is really not unattractive. Now we are praying we might stay here until after Christmas and have ordered a small tree.

Some of the Red Cross girls have been to Paris on business and return with reports of great lack of fuel. One said it was much too cold in the hotel to write letters so she spent most of her time in bed trying to keep warm. It reminded me of your story of continued lack of fuel in Belgium in WW I and the way you all hung around an oil lamp trying to get warm …

I hope to get some pictures of the country around here. The hedgerows of very tall trees with branches only at the top are perfectly beautiful silhouetted against one of these very rare sunsets. It's usually raining …

How are Loppy and Missy [two of Elizabeth's Afghan hounds]?

Much love,

Catherine R.[1]

18 Mar. '45

Dear Miss White,

When I came back the other day I found your letter of Feb. 18 and one of Dec. 8 and today your package with the olives and one bar of that delightful soap. I've been eating olives all day. I just couldn't wait for a better occasion. Thank you so very much for all of them. I'm saving the soap as sachet for my clothes closet. Both Ruth Frisch and I will smell delightfully sweet …

The cow pasture has made us appreciate plain living so much more. Even though our last [station] was in one of the most modern and beautiful hospitals outside Paris with elegant nurses headquarters in comparison to ours I was delighted to get back to my little tile-floored apartment where the sun pours in thru the French windows. The vine that covers the wall is beginning to bud and I believe is a lace vine like yours. With a few more days as warm and sunny as today we shall all be out planting a garden.

Your tulips are probably in bloom by now. Are they as lovely as last year? Your Dec. 8 letter had the picture of the Tamarisk in color. They are so lovely. It reminded me so much of them last spring with those lovely deep purple iris. Maybe next spring I shall see them again.

The other day I had a patient and with a name so familiar I couldn't resist asking where his home was—San Acacio St., Santa Fe, and the name … Rodriguez. He was just awarded the purple heart for being injured doing a very good piece of work up in Germany … After he learned I had lived in Santa Fe he followed me around like a pet pup for the entire two days I was there. His injury is not too serious and he will probably be going back to duty before long.

24 Sept. '45

Dear Miss White,

Your letter came at just the right time. It was waiting when I returned from Switzerland on Thursday and was a much needed tonic after those seven heavenly days and then dropping back into this dull routine. I think I've never enjoyed a trip more. The contrast is so great it is like living in different worlds. I must go back again sometime.

While at Montreaux I went through the Castle of Chillon. Most interesting but frightfully depressing. I met a young Lt. there who had to dash thru and get a train back to Italy and as is usual in almost any conversation, "Where are you from?" popped up and when I told him Santa Fe he wondered if I knew the White sisters there who had kennels and collected Dogs for Defense. He said he had had a delightful correspondence with one of the girls but had never had the pleasure of meeting her. Perhaps you might know him. His name is Kulp and was in the New York office.

In the Army he is head of the Canine Corps in the Italian sector but is now ready to return to the States. He said I should be sure and tell you that the dogs did superior work, several were wounded but only one was lost and that was by our own mortar fire. I should love to have heard more about them but he hadn't time.

The prospect of having my old job back delights me more than I can say. There is nothing I would rather do when and if ever my "Uncle" decides to release me. You are taking a great chance as I have become extremely allergic to home life and home cooking. Last week I'm sure I gained ten pounds. After a month at your house I should be absolutely worthless …

El Delirio must be perfectly beautiful about now with all the purple and gold of the fall asters and chamisa and those wonderful poplars turning. And at night the stars that come almost within reach. Even Switzerland didn't have that. I can hardly wait to see it again.

Much love,

Catherine R.

Elizabeth's letters to Catherine filled her in on the news:

10/7/44

Dearest Catherine,

Loppy and Zara have both been dreadfully ill. Knut and Scott and I nursed them 24 hours a day. Loppy is now as good as new. But my darling Zara is dead and buried. She is the one I loved the best. I shall never have another like her.

Ever thine,

Elizabeth

Elizabeth White (left) and the Dogs for Defense, ca. 1944.

I went out to view the planets, Venus, Jupiter as big as a tomato—with the skyscope ... I am much better now. Weigh 85 lbs. (1/15/45)

Mrs. Wilson brought me fi lb. of real butter from their place near Hobbs where they have a cow. That's the first taste of real butter we've had in six months. Isn't butter delicious!! I wonder when we shall get back to the American Standard of Living. I never did think the New Deal was a good substitute. (1/26/45)

The atom bomb scientists emerged from their silence this week and told us something about their work. We had a meeting at the Laboratory of Anthropology. It was plain to see that they are worried about the future. So come home soon! They have made an "Association of Los Alamos Scientists" (ALAS is what they call themselves. Most appropriate!) to tell the world what to expect if the United Nations organization doesn't work. We were shown a colored movie of the bomb blast over Hiroshima. The top of the mushroom was snow white and the stem all the colors of the rainbow. Have you seen pictures of it? (11/29/45)

As if to acknowledge the tragedy embedded in the rainbow, Elizabeth's Christmas card for 1945 depicted a Japanese Virgin Mary and Christ child.

Elizabeth contributed to the war effort in whatever way she could. She offered her kennels to Dogs for Defense, bought and sold war bonds, and sent Catherine books for the hospital library in Normandy. Since there was a weight limit on how much an individual could send, she had each of the dogs "send" books. She donated $5,000 to the Brun's Hospital Library in Santa Fe for books. She also offered her billiard room to the Navy recruiters in Santa Fe. "But," said Catherine, "it was cold and she barred them from having girls over there. It didn't last."

Catherine returned to Santa Fe and Elizabeth White's employ at the end of 1945 to find that she had been appointed head of Elizabeth's latest project, the Garcia Street Club. Earlier that year, Elizabeth had purchased the home of Hilario Garcia, believed to be the original home site of the family for which Garcia Street is named. She built Mr. Garcia a new house, moved him into it, and then rehabilitated the old house's mud floors and sagging roof and added a platform stage. In November she announced the formation of the Neighborhood Association, Inc., and the Garcia Street Club came into being to provide organized play and craft activities for neighborhood children who had no playground nearby. A statement of purpose appeared in the Santa Fe paper:

> The Garcia St. Club at 569 Garcia St. will seek to help each child to cherish and appreciate the values of his inheritance and that of others, thus establishing a general sense of fair play. It is hoped that the supervised playground and indoor activities will meet the urgent needs and be of special benefit to the children living in the vicinity of Garcia St.
>
> The success of the club house depends not only on the children and director, but on the parents also. Primarily a playground with suitable equipment, it can also be a meeting place for the entire neighborhood, a center of social activities, of plays, dances, and parties.[2]

Boys and girls of the Garcia Street Club making street signs, 1947.

Elizabeth sat on the club's Board of Directors from its inception throughout the 1950s. Over the years the other directors included some of her closest friends: John and Faith Meem, Gustave and Jane Baumann, and the Misses Brownell and Howland, who had started the Shipley School for Girls in Pennsylvania and were known to her from her Bryn Mawr days.

Photos from the early days at the Garcia Street Club show children engaged in activities such as woodworking, tin working, sewing, cooking, drawing, and dancing. Elizabeth involved many of her social circle in club activities. Archaeologist Sylvanus Morley, dancer Jacques Cartier, and others taught or lectured at the club. Will Shuster led a mask-making workshop. Sidney White, an art instructor just back from the war in the South Pacific, brought pictures of tropical birds to help the children to learn to draw. A photographer friend showed the children pioneering work in time-lapse photography of flower growth. Jane and Gustave Baumann gave liberally of their time: Gus put on puppet shows using some of the marvelous marionettes he carved of local figures and folk characters, and Jane collected the ends of weavings for

Elizabeth cutting a celebratory cake at the Garcia Street Club, 1947.

quilts that the children made for war orphans. Elizabeth herself taught piano for a while, charging two cents a lesson, "so they should know that it costs." The stage was used for theatrical productions of *Cinderella, Peter Pan, Snow White and the Seven Dwarfs,* and *Peter and the Wolf* and for Fiesta parties, dances, and the traditional New Mexico Christmas folk play, *Los Pastores.*

The clubhouse also served as a center for adults. Sylvanus Morley, whose expeditions Elizabeth had been supporting for thirty years, gave an illustrated slide talk, in Spanish, on "The History of the Most Illustrious of the Ancient Civilizations—The Mayas of Central America." (Neighbors later chuckled to Catherine that Morley's Spanish was "unique.") Crafts classes for adults were offered in the evenings. One class, dedicated to the revival of colonial New Mexican *colcha* embroidery, was so popular with neighborhood women that the local men became envious and asked that the woodworking shop be open to them in the evenings. In addition, groups such as the Rotary Club, Quakers, Santa Fe Choral Society, the Little Theater, World Federalists, Photographer's Club, Chess Club, and Alcoholics Anonymous used the space for meetings.

The club's primary role, however, was as a children's center, providing interesting activities for the local children and going outside the immediate neighborhood to include others. The children put on parties for girls from the St. Vincent Orphanage and for boys from the Boys' Ranch, a school for troubled adolescents in Bosque Farms, New Mexico. This kind of outreach was part of an ethos that Elizabeth White wished to foster. A Garcia Street Club pamphlet set forth the philosophy: "'Gangsterism' is the destructive form which can be prevented by 'Belonging.' With the knowledge that one belongs to a Club that stands for construction and fair play no matter what neglect or rejection may be the lot of a boy or girl, that sense of belonging gives him the security which anti-dotes gangsterism."[3] The Garcia Street Club continues to operate as a preschool child care program. Many of the parents who bring their children there today went there as youngsters themselves.

Elizabeth was a member of the Old Santa Fe Association (OSFA) and financed a number of its projects. The OSFA was originally created to oppose the plan of the Federated Women's Club of Texas to build a summer colony outside of

Santa Fe. Aware of the fragility of the community, the OSFA set itself a worthy task: "To preserve and maintain the ancient landmarks, historical structures and traditions of Old Santa Fe; to guide its growth and development in such a way as to sacrifice as little as possible of that unique charm, born of age, tradition and environment which are the priceless assets and heritage of Old Santa Fe."[4] Among their efforts was the preservation of El Zaguan, the historic Canyon Road home said to have once belonged to pioneer anthropologist Adolph Bandelier. Elizabeth was also a member of the New Mexico Roadside Council, whose motto was "Safety and Beauty for Our Highways—Control the Billboards."

In her biography of architect John Gaw Meem, Beatrice Chauvenet writes, "The preservationist who elects to save a living culture must be content to see it change in the hands of its new inheritors."[5] This is easier said than done. When the city considered paving Garcia Street and other streets in the former De Vargas Development, Elizabeth White attended the hearings to protest. Catherine Rayne remembers,

> They would announce a street. She would get up and walk down to the front with her straight spine. It was the straightest spine you've ever seen. "Mr. Mayor. Council members. I should like to protest the paving of Corrales," or whatever street it was. They'd huddle and then someone would say, "That section, Miss White, has been sold. You don't own that any more." Then she would walk back and sit down. There would be complete silence. Because she owned so much land she had a lot of protesting to do. They'd announce another street. Again, she would get up and walk to the front. They would go through the same ceremony every time.

Another of Elizabeth's interests, the Spanish Colonial Arts Society of New Mexico, was (and is) dedicated to the preservation and revitalization of Spanish Colonial arts, including the rough-hewn, simple, and beautiful furniture arts. Hispanic scholars, beginning with Aurelio Espinosa in 1915, had begun to document Spanish heritage in New Mexico at the same time that Anglo anthropologists were becoming enamored of the region. At the turn of

Elizabeth and Catherine on board the Andrea Doria, *ca. 1953.*

the century, Eastern immigrants to New Mexico provided the impetus for much of the preservation of Spanish and Indian arts and crafts; Elizabeth's circle was an important part of this movement.

During the last twenty years of Elizabeth's life, she and Catherine became great travelers. They went to the Middle East, Europe, and India. They went to Stratford, Ontario, for the Shakespeare Festival each summer for four years ("to avoid celebrating Elizabeth's birthday," according to Catherine) and traveled to the North Cape of Norway to witness the midnight sun. Another trip took them to the Roman ruins of Baalbeck, Lebanon, where Elizabeth's paternal grandparents had gone on their honeymoon and had their photo taken standing on the remains of the ancient temple of Bacchus. Elizabeth wanted her picture taken at the same spot—an unusual request, as she generally disliked being photographed.

Travel had an animating effect on Elizabeth. During one particularly rough ocean crossing, Catherine was very seasick. "The ship was rocking and rolling. Elizabeth would come back to our cabin from the deck with the greatest amount of gossip about the news of the day—the steward broke his leg and

The summer palace, Udaipur, India.

a stewardess had a gash in her forehead. But she clung to the ropes and made the trip without incident." Indeed, Elizabeth seems to have been motivated by the challenges of hardship. In the mid-1950s one of her friends, just returned from the massive red stone ruins of Petra, in Jordan, reported that it was a hard trip down on horseback or donkey and that she doubted Elizabeth could make it. Within a few days Elizabeth had made plans to visit the site.

While in Udaipur, India, in 1966, Elizabeth and Catherine stayed at the Maharaja's summer palace, a magnificent structure floating in an artificial lake. A photo shows the two riding atop an elephant, the tiny, eighty-eight-year-old Elizabeth holding firmly onto the edges of the wicker box in which they perched. During this trip, however, Elizabeth became very ill with pneumonia. Upon returning to the US, she learned that she had suffered a heart attack. Thereafter she was bedridden much of the time until her death six years later.

Throughout the last twenty-five years of her life Elizabeth remained a generous philanthropist. Wherever she traveled, she collected folk instruments and donated them to the Museum of International Folk Art in Santa Fe. She gave gifts of folk and fine art to museums in New Mexico and elsewhere.[6] She kept up her connections with the political world as well, contributing to the Republican Party of Santa Fe and to the NAACP legal defense and education fund. (Horace White had been an early supporter of the NAACP.) She also gave to individuals in a direct and personal way, establishing a scholarship fund for musicians through the Santa Fe Sinfonietta and sending monthly remittances to, among many others, a person her father had befriended and a woman in Albuquerque who had cancer.

One of the causes dearest to her heart was the Indian Arts Fund. According to Marge Lambert,

> She worked closely with the early caretakers and guiding forces on the Indian Arts Fund—Stanley Stubbs, Kenneth Chapman, and Harry Mera—and was the most knowledgeable next to them. Miss White gave of herself. She worked with the collection. She thought about where there was a gap in the collections. She had an intellectual interest in it, as distinct from only giving money. She gave many of the finest things in our collection. She gave out of wanting to do things. She never wanted recognition.[7]

Elizabeth also loved playing hostess to interesting guests. Boaz Long, who headed the School of American Research from 1948 to 1956 and had served as American consul in Ecuador and El Salvador, asked her to entertain visiting dignitaries from time to time. She was no stranger to this role. When the American Anthropological Society held its annual meeting in Albuquerque in 1948, she hosted the entire group for lunch at El Delirio. On other occasions she entertained a group of Los Alamos atomic scientists, including Robert Oppenheimer and Enrico Fermi, and hosted the Western Writers Conference at Santa Fe's historic La Fonda. Among the guests at El Delirio over the years were Joy Adamson (author of *Born Free*), Mabel Dodge Luhan, Agatha Christie and her husband, the noted archaeologist Max Mallowan, and Sir Hubert Wilkins, who had rescued Kurt Gustafson in the Antarctic.

And then there were the parties. If Martha had been the instigator in the early years of El Delirio, Catherine Rayne carried on the tradition admirably. "When Elizabeth got low I'd say, 'How about a party?' and she'd pep right up," Catherine recalls. At a 1953 party that coincided with the coronation of Queen Elizabeth II, the guests wore costumes of the first Elizabethan era. Queen Elizabeth I was none other than Amelia Elizabeth White. Writer Dorothy Stewart

The New York Room in the 1960s.

came as a Maharani dressed in a purple sari. Margretta Dietrich and Marshall McCune showed up in ermine capes, which Elizabeth insisted they wear throughout the evening. "Doesn't she know it's hot as Hades under these?" Dietrich complained to Catherine.

Another party was held in 1956 to dedicate the summer house, or gazebo, where Martha's ashes were buried. Candles in red sanctuary cups lined the road that wound from the chapel to the gazebo, and the terraces too were lighted with farolitos. During the 1960s Elizabeth hosted gala events for composer Igor Stravinsky, pianists José Iturbi and Claudio Arrau, and guitarist Andres Segovia. John Meem's daughter, Nancy Meem Wirth, describes orchids lining the front hall at El Delirio. "Her parties were occasions of state," Meem said.[8]

Music and books were the other great passions of Elizabeth's later life. When they built their estate, Elizabeth and Martha brought Horace White's library from New York and reconstructed it in Santa Fe. The El Delirio library included numerous first editions, books on dogs, history, bees, oysters, juvenile delinquency, Mayan architecture, natural history, philosophy, anthropology, American history, the Southwest, classics of ancient Greece and Rome, English literature, and modern fiction, and books by Horace White and by Abby

Elizabeth at El Delirio, ca. 1950.

White's father-in-law, William Dean Howells, and her son, William White Howells.

Elizabeth had studied piano as a child and continued playing throughout her life. She also loved live chamber music, for which the chapel at El Delirio provided the perfect setting. She gave her energies faithfully to the Santa Fe Sinfonietta and Choral Society, directed by Hans Lange. "El Delirio was a wonderful place for music," Catherine Rayne reports:

> The large chapel would easily seat seventy-five. On one occasion there were 175 for a supper party which overflowed onto the terrace. The sound of Mozart floating out on the moonlit terrace was especially lovely.
>
> Dr. Lange had returned to a home he had bought in Abiquiu, in northern New Mexico. Toscanini visited him there and did some recordings. He was impressed with the results and declared that adobe was the most perfect material for proper acoustics. Dr. Lange and his wife, pianist Marcella Kossman, later moved down to Santa Fe and he became the director of a small Sinfonietta which he had formed.
>
> Miss White was quite a good pianist and asked Lange if he had a pupil whom she could get to play duets with her. He said, "Why not me?" There followed several musical evenings with duos, trios, or quartets. Eunice Hawskins often played second violin and Randall Davey, the artist and friend of John Sloan, played the cello. What better excuse for a party than to hear the music?

On the day before she died, Elizabeth announced a desire to hear Mozart's *Eine Kleine Nacht Musik*. Catherine lugged a phonograph up to the Gallery from the main house below, but Elizabeth said, "No, I want to hear it *live*." It was a Sunday afternoon and impossible to gather musicians on short notice. She did not get her wish.

Amelia Elizabeth White died on August 28, 1972, her ninety-fourth birthday. A private farewell was held in the chapel of El Delirio. At the public funeral, which took place at the Episcopal Church of Holy Faith in Santa Fe, most of the pallbearers were gardeners at El Delirio. Carlos Garcia, Ben LeDoux, Ignacio Vigil, and Ted Herrera all had tended the grounds that she lived in and loved. One has only to see the gardens, set among the stone terraces made from rocks gathered from the mountains near Las Vegas, New Mexico, to sense the effort that went into bringing color and subtlety to that dry landscape. It was fitting that these men stood up for Miss E. at the end.

Notes

ACKNOWLEDGMENTS

Many people assisted in the creation of this book. My thanks go to anthropologist Molly Mullin, for teaching me to follow my instincts in conducting research; the staff of the School of American Research and the Indian Arts Research Center; Marie Watt and Charlene Teters of the Institute of American Indian Arts; Laura Holt of the Museum of New Mexico's Laboratory of Anthropology; Joni Herren, for sensitive editing of earlier drafts of this book; and Jo Ann Baldinger, who sorted wheat from chaff. William White Howells and William Dean Howells, nephew and grandnephew of Elizabeth White, generously shared their time, their recollections, and many family photographs. Dozens of individuals who knew the White sisters and experienced life at El Delirio were interviewed for this book; I thank them all for their gracious assistance. Thanks also to my friends and family for their support and encouragement.

Finally, Catherine Rayne opened the world of Elizabeth White to me and guided me through it with humor and patience. She cared deeply about this book and believed in my ability to give it shape. Her love for and loyalty to Elizabeth White are woven into every page. To you, Catherine, my greatest thanks.
—*Gregor Stark*

I had long wished to honor the remarkable life and character of my dear friend, Amelia Elizabeth White, who died in 1972. In 1988 I asked another good friend, Gregor Stark, to help me write Miss E.'s story for the benefit of those who had not had the privilege of knowing her and the important role she played in so many aspects of Santa Fe's history. I have known Gregor since he was fifteen, when he helped me in my garden, and I felt confident that he could do justice to his subject.

I am very grateful to the School of American Research Press, particularly director Joan O'Donnell, art director Deborah Flynn, and editor Jo Ann Baldinger, for the care they have taken in producing this tribute to Miss E. I am also grateful to the many people who contributed their memories during the preparation of *El Delirio*. Lastly, my profound thanks go to Gregor Stark for sticking to his dream.
—*E. Catherine Rayne*

ARCHIVAL SOURCES

CR: Catherine Rayne personal papers

CSWR: Center for Southwest Research, University of New Mexico

FCW: Frank C. Wilson Papers, New Mexico State Archives

LAB: Laboratory of Anthropology

NMSA: New Mexico State Archives

SAR: School of American Research

WWH: William White Howells personal papers

Note: All personal interviews were conducted by Gregor Stark between 1992 and 1994.

INTRODUCTION

1. Interview.
2. May 1994, WWH.
3. Interview.

CHAPTER 1: SANTA FE STYLE

1. Paz 1985:24.
2. Nusbaum 1950:162–63.
3. Hewett 1917.
4. Bell n.d.:42–45.
5. This letter, and those that follow between Frank C. Wilson and the White sisters, are in the SAR archives.
6. May 1926, SAR.
7. Deeds of Record, Santa Fe County Clerk.

CHAPTER 2: FORMATIVE YEARS

1. Interview.
2. Logsdon 1971:31.
3. Ibid., 106.
4. White 1895:10.
5. January 1891, WWH.
6. June 1893, WWH.
7. White 1900.
8. James 1907:185.
9. Ibid., 159.
10. Howells 1885:24–25.
11. Bender 1987:193.
12. Abby White's father-in-law, William Dean Howells, wrote to Henry James on 17 March 1912 about a women's suffrage march in New York City: "We shall all be marching in the suffrage procession in May: John's two boys, their two grandfathers, John and his wife, the two White girls and Pilla [Howells' daughter], shouting the battle cry of female freedom" (Howells 1983:16). Ten thousand people reportedly attended the march.
13. Addams 1910.
14. SAR.
15. MRW diaries, CR.
16. WWH papers.
17. March 1918, SAR.
18. August 1919, CR.

CHAPTER 3: INDIAN LANDS AND INDIAN HEALTH

1. Kate Chapman to Margaret McKittrick, 29 April 1931, FCW.
2. EAIA 1930:9.
3. Philp 1986:8.
4. Kelly 1983:230ff.
5. NMAIA 1921–22:4.
6. Ibid., 6–7.
7. AIDA brief, p. 12; FCW.
8. Ibid., 14.
9. FCW.
10. Ibid.
11. Kelly 1983:230.
12. Interview.
13. January 1924, SAR.
14. Public No. 253, Sec. 11, 68th Congress, approved 7 June 1924, p. 5.
15. Sergeant 1923:121.
16. This letter and the following exchange are at CSWR.
17. White 1924:311.
18. All-Pueblo Council Meeting 1924:24–25, John Collier Papers, CSWR.
19. FCW.
20. Ibid.
21. Ibid.
22. SAR.
23. Interview.
24. SAR.
25. EAIA Bulletin 24:3, LAB.

26. Schackel 1992:69.
27. SAR.
28. December 1931, SAR.
29. November 1932, SAR.
30. SAR.

CHAPTER 4: INDIAN ART

1. Spinden 1931:6.
2. Morris 1893:10–11.
3. See Brody 1997 for a history of the modern Pueblo painting tradition.
4. Glassie 1989:244.
5. April 1932, SAR.
6. Ishauu reported a net loss of $3,870 in 1923. At the time, Elizabeth White had invested approximately $6,000 in the shop. Monthly sales for September and October 1932 were $147 and $470, respectively; for March and April 1933, they were $506 and $518.
7. SAR.
8. April 1930, SAR.
9. SAR.
10. Exposition of Indian Tribal Arts 1931:21.
11. Octavio Paz (1985:102) offers an interesting insight into the different dynamics of Protestant and Catholic contact with the Indians. "Anyone who knows the treatment of the Indians by the military will laugh at this hypothesis, but the fate of the Indians would have been very different if it had not been for the Church. I am not thinking only of its struggle to improve living conditions and to organize them in a more just and Christian manner, but also of the opportunity that baptism offered them to form a part of one social order and one religion. This possibility of belonging to a living order, even if it was at the bottom of the social pyramid, was cruelly denied to the Indians by the Protestants of New England."
12. Exposition of Indian Tribal Arts 1931:7.
13. Ibid., v. 2.
14. December 1931, SAR.
15. Interview.

16. February 1932, SAR.
17. NAIA 1935.
18. January 1924, SAR.
19. November 1932, SAR.
20. April 1931, SAR. Rorick later wrote a book, *Navaho Trading Days*, under the name Elizabeth Hegemann (1963).
21. March 1932, SAR.
22. Cousins, n.d.:33. By permission of Bill Cousins and Ruth Hobbs.
23. Bernstein 1993:54.
24. April 1934, SAR. Dietrich noted that, in addition to Chapman's lectures, "Dr. Harry Mera [gave] two Mr. James MacMillan and Mr. Norman McGee each gave one, Miss Olive Rush and Miss Dorothy Dunn of the Indian School had the lesson on painting and Mrs. Frances Newcomb came from Nava to talk on Navajo Sandpaintings."
25. Examination for Indian Fair Judges, 19 April 1934, LAB.
26. KMC lecture notes, c. 1934, LAB.
27. KMC lecture notes, c. 1936, LAB.
28. September 1933, SAR.
29. SAR.
30. ESS, John Collier Papers, CSWR.
31. NAIA 1935:11–15.

CHAPTER 5: A CIRCLE OF FRIENDS

1. *Santa Fe New Mexican*, 11 April 1914:1.
2. WWH.
3. Burnhouse 1975:93.
4. May 1930, LAB.
5. SAR.
6. SAR.
7. November 1931, SAR.
8. SAR.
9. November 1930, SAR.
10. Kraft and Sloan 1981:32ff.
11. "Talk on Art," 29 July 1932:2–3, SAR.
12. Brooks 1955:159.
13. Sloan 1939:325.
14. Interview.
15. *Santa Fe New Mexican*, 2 July 1929.
16. SAR.

17. Evans 1991:9.
18. Interview.
19. Bud Kelly interview.
20. Interview.
21. *Santa Fe New Mexican*, 31 August 1935:2.
22. Jones 1934:4, 5.
23. May 1994, WWH.
24. Fanny Osgood 1905, SAR.
25. MRW diaries, CR.
26. These gifts went to the Albright Gallery, Buffalo Fine Arts Academy, the American Museum of Natural History, the Art Students League of New York, the Artists Fair and Bazaar, the Boston Museum of Fine Arts, the Boy Scouts of America, Manhattan Council, the Children's Art Centre of University Settlement House, the Cincinnati Art Museum, the Cleveland Museum of Art, the Columbus Gallery of Fine Arts, the Corcoran Gallery, the Cranbrook Institute of Science, the Detroit Institute of Art, the Lenox Hill Neighborhood Association, New York Hospital, and the Peabody Museum at Harvard.
27. *Miami Herald*, 29 February 1938.

CHAPTER 6: FURTHER ADVENTURES

1. The following quoted letters are from Catherine Rayne's personal papers.
2. *Santa Fe New Mexican*, 7 February 1946.
3. CR.
4. Chauvenet 1985:21.
5. Ibid., x.
6. Among the many institutions that benefited from Elizabeth White's generosity were the Indian Arts Fund (paintings by Oqwa Pi, Awa Tsireh, Otis Polelonema, Velino Herrera, a Zuni altar piece, and pottery from Mesa Verde and Chaco Canyon); the Museum of New Mexico (a wood sculpture, "San Jose y Maria," by Lopez of Cordoba, New Mexico tinwork, and paintings by John Sloan, William Penhallow Henderson, and Olive Rush); the Palace of the Governors (an antique map from 1674); the Cleveland Museum of Art (John Sloan's "Woman's Work"); the Whitney Museum of American Art (Sloan's "Dolly with Black Bow"); the Museum of Natural History (slate totems, pipes, and ivory and bone boxes); and the New York Public Library, to which she gave a set of Gustave Baumann woodcuts in 1965, in Martha's memory.
7. Interview.
8. Interview.

PICTURE CREDITS

Unless otherwise noted, all photographs are from the collections of E. Catherine Rayne and the School of American Research.

ABBREVIATIONS

IARC Indian Arts Research Center at SAR
MNM Museum of New Mexico
NMSRCA New Mexico State Records Center and Archives
SAR School of American Research

4, Bachrach; **6 top,** Herbert Lotz; **12,** T. Harmon Parkhurst; **16 top,** T. Harmon Parkhurst, courtesy MNM, neg. no. 2834; **16 bottom, 17, 21, 25,** T. Harmon Parkhurst; **35,** courtesy William White Howells; **42 top,** Jesse Nusbaum, courtesy MNM, neg. no. 139438; **48,** T. Harmon Parkhurst; **49,** IARC P.149; **51,** courtesy NMSRCA, neg. no. 33019; **67,** IARC 1978.1.311; **77 top,** Wesley Bradfield, courtesy MNM, neg. no. 42213; **77 bottom,** SAR 1978-1-214; **80,** SAR T.2; **86,** Jesse L. Nusbaum(?), courtesy MNM, neg. no. 13311; **89 top,** Cross Studio, courtesy MNM, neg. no. 1498; **89 bottom,** SAR T.175; **92,** IARC S.578; **97 top,** Jesse Nusbaum; **102 clockwise from top left,** Will Connell, courtesy MNM, neg. no. 59752; Wyatt Davis, courtesy Whitney Museum of American Art; courtesy Witter Bynner Foundation for Poetry; courtesy Ann Baumann; **132,** Tyler Dingee.

References

Addams, Jane
1910   The Modern City and the Municipal Franchise for Women. In *Women's Suffrage, Arguments and Results.* Reprint, New York: Kraus Reprint Co., 1971.

Bell, David
n.d.   Biography of William P. Henderson. Unpublished manuscript.

Bender, Thomas
1987   *New York Intellect: A History of Intellectual Life in New York City from 1750 to the Beginnings of Our Time.* New York: Alfred A. Knopf.

Bernstein, Bruce
1993   From Indian Fair to Indian Market. *El Palacio* 99(3):14–18, 47–54.

Brody, J. J.
1997   *Pueblo Indian Painting: Tradition and Modernism in New Mexico, 1900–1930.* Santa Fe: School of American Research Press.

Brooks, Van Wyck
1955   *John Sloan: A Painter's Life.* New York: E. P. Dutton

Burnhouse, Robert L.
1975   *Pursuit of the Ancient Maya: Some Archaeologists of Yesterday.* Albuquerque: University of New Mexico Press.

Chauvenet, Beatrice
1985   *John Gaw Meem, Pioneer in Historic Preservation.* Santa Fe: Historic Santa Fe Foundation/Museum of New Mexico Press.

Cousins, Bill
n.d.   Trading Memoirs. Unpublished manuscript.

EAIA (Eastern Association on Indian Affairs)
1930   The American Indian—A National Obligation. Bulletin 19.
1924–34 Various field reports and bulletins.

Exposition of Indian Tribal Arts, Inc.
1931   *Introduction to American Indian Art.* 2 v. Frederick Webb Hodge, Herbert Joseph Spinden, and Oliver LaFarge, editors. New York.

Evans, Clay
1991   A Cowboy Rides to the Great Beyond. *Santa Fe Reporter*, 6–12 March.

Glassie, Henry
1989   *The Spirit of Folk Art: The Girard Collection at the Museum of International Folk Art.* New York: Harry N. Abrams.

Hegemann, Elizabeth Compton
1963   *Navaho Trading Days.* Albuquerque: University of New Mexico Press.

Hewett, Edgar Lee
1917   Santa Fe in 1926. *El Palacio* 4(1):23–27 (January).

Howells, William Dean
1885   *The Rise of Silas Lapham.* Reprint. New York: Collier Books, 1962.
1983   *Selected Letters,* v. 6, 1912–1920. Edited and annotated by William M. Gibson and Christoph K. Lohmann. Boston: Twayne Publishers.

James, Henry
1907   *The American Scene.* Reprint, New York: Horizon Press, 1967.

Jones, Arthur Frederick
1934   Erin's Famous Hounds Finding Greater Glory at Rathmullan. *American Kennel Gazette* 51(5) (May).

Kelly, Lawrence
1983   *The Assault on Assimilation: John Collier and the Origins of Indian Policy Reform.* Albuquerque: University of New Mexico Press.

Kraft, James, and Helen Farr Sloan
1981   *John Sloan in Santa Fe.* Washington, DC: Smithsonian Institution.

Logsdon, Joseph
1971   *Horace White, Nineteenth Century Liberal.* Westport, CT: Greenwood Publishing Co.

Morris, William
1893   *Arts and Crafts Essays.* Reprint. New York and London: Garland Publishing, Inc., 1977.

NAIA (National Association on Indian Affairs)
1935   Contemporary Southwestern Indian Arts and Crafts. Bulletin no. 23. Santa Fe.

NMAIA (New Mexico Association on Indian Affairs)
1921–22 Annual Report. Santa Fe.

Nusbaum, Jesse L.
1950   Vay Morley and the Santa Fe Style. In *Morleyana: A Collection of Writings in Memoriam, Sylvanus Griswold Morley, 1883–1948.* Santa Fe: Museum of New Mexico and School of American Research.

Paz, Octavio
1985   *The Labyrinth of Solitude and Other Writings.* Translated by Lysander Kemp, Yara Milos, and Rachael Phillips Belash. New York: Grove Weidenfeld.

Philp, Kenneth, ed.
1986   *Indian Self-Rule.* Salt Lake City: Howe Brothers.

Santa Fe New Mexican
1914–46 Various issues.

Schackel, Sandra
1992   *Social Housekeepers: Women Shaping
        Public Policy in New Mexico*. Albu-
        querque: University of New Mexico
        Press.

Sergeant, Elizabeth Shepley
1923   Communication—The Plight of
        the Pueblos. *New Republic* 37(473)
        (26 December).

Sloan, John
1939   *The Gist of Art*. New York:
        American Artists Group, Inc.

White, Amelia Elizabeth
1900   The Mouse. *Bryn Mawr Fortnightly
        Philistine* 9:3.
1924   A Response to Elizabeth Shepley
        Sergeant. *New Republic*, 13 February,
        p. 311.

White, Horace
1895   *Money and Banking, Illustrated by
        American History*. Boston: Ginn
        and Co.

Index